JOY Maker?

To Diana,
 a wonderful &
beautiful young
 lady!
 God bless!
  Carla Christian

Are You a JOY Maker?

Karla Christian

Are You a Joy Maker?

by Karla Christian

Cover design by Laura Jurek
All photos used by permission

Copyright © 2010, Karla Christian

All Scripture quotations in this book are from the King James Version of the Bible unless otherwise identified.

All rights reserved. No portion of this publication may be reproduced, stored in an electronic system, or transmitted in any form or by any means, electronic, mechanical, photocopy, recording, or otherwise, without the prior permission of Word Aflame Press. Brief quotations may be used in literary reviews.

Printed in United States of America

WORD AFLAME PRESS
8855 Dunn Road, Hazelwood, MO 63042
www.pentecostalpublishing.com

Library of Congress Cataloging-in-Publication Data

Christian, Karla, 1957-
 Are you a joy maker? / by Karla Christian.
   p. cm.
 ISBN 978-0-7577-4028-2
 1. Joy--Religious aspects--Christianity. I. Title.
 BV4647.J68C495 2010
 241'.4--dc22
                              2010033380

Dedication

I would like to dedicate this writing endeavor to my incredible family, who has provided the majority of my stories and inspiration.

My wonderful and awesome husband, Mark Christian, who kindly reminds me of the spiritual side of things. Thanks for making our life together so marvelous and grand.

My beautiful daughter, Kara and her husband, Bobby McCool, who continue to "make me proud" for their dedication and commitment to the work of God.

My beautiful daughter, Courtney, who brings much joy to everyone she is around. Thank you for the comic relief you have provided when stress seemed unbearable.

My beautiful daughter, Kalee, who has never failed to bring energy into any atmosphere when she "charges" into a room.

And I need not forget my beloved mother, Wanda Smart, who keeps believing in me.

To my awesome sister, Vicki, who has definitely been an inspiration and brought that much needed laughter to my life.

To the remainder of my family, the Christian Clan, the Hapke Household, the Tivis Tribe, and the Stewart Side, it has been a pleasure to spend all those wonderful reunions and holidays with you all.

My amazing family has definitely been "Joy Makers" in my life.

I also want to dedicate this book to two of the most incredible people I have ever known, Pastor and Sister J. T. Pugh. How I will miss them! My small effort at writing seems rather inconsequential when compared to their wonderful ministries, leadership, and lives. The time we spent as their assistants in Odessa, Texas, was one of the greatest privileges we could have ever been afforded. We will forever count it a high honor to have had them as our mentors and friends.

J.T. and Bessie Pugh

Special Thanks

Thank you to all the wonderful friends who have blessed our lives just by allowing us their friendships.

Jerry and Phyllis Jones—Thank you for giving me so many great ideas and for being there to give me the nudge I needed at the perfect time. We will never forget the impact you have had on our lives from the time we preached (or rather Mark preached) that revival at your awesome church and you so kindly took up a special offering to honor us on our first wedding anniversary.

Terry and Pam Pugh—Thank you for the laughter and the kindness you have extended to us through the years. And, of course, the wisdom and candor you have shared have offered great talking points as well.

Rick and Renee Flowers—Thank you for being there for us in the storms of life. And especially my dear Renee, what would I have done without my childhood friend?

Darrell and Carol Johns—Thank God we had the chance to spend all those awesome years with you in the Youth Division. We did learn a lot and enjoyed each other's company in the midst of our treks to the hospital with our children.

Thank you to the wonderful church family at the First United Pentecostal Church of Leesville, Louisiana, who has so graciously welcomed us with incredible kindness. We are honored and privileged to serve with you in the kingdom of God. What an exciting and awesome time we are having!

Thanks to all who have filled our lives with your friendship. I so wish I could name every one of you. We have been blessed beyond measure by the joy of friends. We love you and thank God for you.

Thanks to all the brilliant staff at Word Aflame Press for your expert assistance in handling the production of this book, especially Reverend Robin Johnston and his capable assistant, Donna Sample. I would so like to call everyone's name, but am not quite certain who all contributed to the final product. Suffice it to say, thank you from the deep of my heart.

A sincere thanks to Renita Weeks of Total Betty Photography, Inc. for her expert skills in making me look as well as can be expected and for the incredible backgrounds she introduced me to at Hodges Gardens.

A special thanks to everyone whose stories fill the pages of this book. You have inspired me to be a better person by your experiences and will inspire others as well when they read about them.

And last, but not least, I give grateful thanks to the Lord of lords and King of kings. There is nothing greater in this life than being able to serve You!

Contents

Preface	11
Interlude 1: A Kodak Moment	15
Interlude 2: Are You in the Picture?	21
Interlude 3: Making the Right Choice	27
Interlude 4: Not My Day	33
Interlude 5: Life Is Just Not Fair	45
Interlude 6: The Natural Thing to Do	53
Interlude 7: Making History	61
Interlude 8: Busy, Busy, Busy	71
Interlude 9: I've Got Confidence	79
Interlude 10: Just Needing a Little Attention	85
Interlude 11: Not Another School Function	89
Interlude 12: I'm Not Perfect	95
Interlude 13: A Friend Indeed	101
Interlude 14: What's It Worth to You?	109
Interlude 15: That's All That Matters	119
Interlude 16: Reach out and Touch	127
Interlude 17: Who Do You Think You Are?	133
Interlude 18: In a Fog	139
Interlude 19: Shut My Mouth	145
Interlude 20: Oh Happy Day	151
Interlude 21: I Want My Joy Back	159
Interlude 22: What's Your Story?	165

Celebrating with Mom on her 80th birthday

The daughters, Kara and Kalee

PREFACE

I was enjoying a much-desired visit with my sister. Rarely do we have occasion to sit and visit since we live miles apart from each other and our families and responsibilities seem to require so much of our attention.

Vicki was bringing me up to date on things in her life, and I was communicating my happenings as well. Since my sister and I love to dramatize stories in order to bring about some laughter, we were doing just that—laughing at some description of a recent happening.

Her little grandson sat on the floor playing with his toys. We started our laughter regimen, and up he came, running to us with a smile on his face. He placed one little hand on Vicki's knee and one little hand on my knee, and with that precious grin on his face, looked from one to the other. We had stopped for a moment to observe his antics, and our laughter subsided. Then he just threw back his head and started laughing, trying to help us start laughing again. He came running to us because he loved the sound of our laughter and wanted to be a part of it.

◌ Are You a Joy Maker?

Little Alex is a joy maker. Even though he did not understand exactly what was going on, he wanted to be a part of it because he loved to laugh. Even though a small little dude, he had already found out what laughter can do for you. He wanted to be right in the middle of it if he could.

While sitting on Vicki's couch watching the actions of little Alex, I came up with the idea for this book, "Are You a Joy Maker?" He was definitely a joy maker. He might be playing contentedly on the floor with his own toys, but upon hearing us laugh, he knew he wanted to be a part of it. This little guy always brought joy to his family. If we became quiet or serious, he would try to make us laugh with his funny behavior and antics. He was a joy maker.

I Googled the word *makers*, and it brought up some neat information. The first two words in one explanation paragraph caught my attention: "Like experiencers." So, makers most likely love to experience the things of life. This article said that makers express themselves and experience the world by working on it, whether it is building a house, raising children, or fixing a car, and have enough skill and energy to carry out their projects successfully. Oh, that sounds wonderful! Especially having skill and energy!

But much more important than having skill and energy is having the joy of the Lord flowing abundantly in our lives. Each day that I live, I want to find

Preface

the joy God has available for my life and "carry out my project successfully." Like little Alex, I may have to walk across the room to get involved, or I may have to paste on a smile when I don't feel like smiling. Whatever the case, I want to be a joy maker for those with whom I come in contact day by day. The loudest message we may ever preach to those around us is the life we live before them.

I do realize that this book can never be used in place of the Bible or as a commentary or a dissertation, but perhaps each chapter you read can be referred to as your daily interlude—a simple, intervening space of dramatic entertainment. I probably would not even go so far as to say dramatic. However, if it helps you as a reader to find a bit of joy in your otherwise stressful and mundane existence, or as a brief respite from the cares of life, my joy will be complete, especially, if I have accomplished what I have set out to do, and that is become a joy maker. I trust perusing one of these interludes will inspire you to become a joy maker for others. I have taken some well-known phrases as titles for these brief interludes, which I hope will enhance the enjoyment of this book even more. Now, are you ready to become a joy maker?

Are You a Joy Maker?

*Alex Grooms, my
great nephew*

You may be only one person in the world, but you may also be the world to one person.
—Unknown

Do what you can, with what you have, where you are.
—Theodore Roosevelt

Interlude 1

A Kodak Moment

A soft evening of fading sunlight. A fine looking family sitting on a quaint park bench overlooking a lake that reflects the sinking sun. Smiling children wiggling in excitement at the prospect of throwing pebbles into the water. My four-year old-nephew took in this magnificent picture of some of their friends enjoying the evening, and in his small childish lingo, looked up at his mom and said, "Looky dhere, Mudder! It's a Kodat moment."

Wouldn't it be wonderful if life was a continuous Kodak moment? A moment of near perfection to savor continuously. Just the thought fills me with happiness.

Unfortunately, as we all know, that may not be the way life always is. I remember hearing a song as a child by a famous singer that said, "That's life! That's what all the people say. You're riding high in April, but shot down in May." I am not certain what kind of life the man led, but he certainly had a concept of what life can sometimes be.

◌⃝ Are You a Joy Maker?

I am reminded of a song my husband and I performed with puppets during some of our memorable years of evangelizing. We sang the song at the end of one of our presentations about Mr. Grump. Mr. Grump was an old-man puppet with no teeth and a balding head. He hated kids and did not want them around his house. However, they befriended him by doing chores and helping him, and they eventually won over Mr. Grump. They all joined together at the end and sang, "Life is made of ups and downs, Some days we smile, some days we frown, but every day we wear a crown, because we're kids of the King. La, la, la, la, la, la, la, la." (I really enjoyed it when we reached the "la la" part.)

Yes, life is made of ups and downs—even if you are a child of the King. God has not promised us that the road we travel will be easy, but He has promised that He would be with us, no matter what comes our way. John 16:33 says, "These things I have spoken unto you, that in me ye might have peace. In the world ye shall have tribulation: but be of good cheer; I have overcome the world."

I remember as a small girl watching as our Pastor Bill Barnes suffered severe headaches. Often during the night Sister Barnes would call my parents to come pray, and I would watch as Brother Barnes would hold his head in such pain he could not respond to anything. In my child's mind, it was difficult for me to understand why our pastor was suffering so when he was a man of God. He should be blessed, not going through such a trial. After he had gone through an intricate surgery to remove the brain tumor they eventually found, I remember talking to Sister Barnes about it and asking her why God allowed this to happen. She kindly told me that she had once heard a sermon that helped her tremendously. She said the context of the sermon was that everything that happens in life is not caused by God or the devil for that matter. It is just simply life.

When I am dealing with "simply life," I often sing a favorite little song of mine which says, "No matter what comes my way, I'll lift my voice and say, Hallelu . . . Hallelu . . . Hallelujah, anyhow!" (Of course, you must hold the "Hallelu" out to really receive the proper lift to your spirits.)

I work part-time for our church organization and enjoy sparring with my co-workers. They never let a moment go by if the chance arises to kid me about being an authoress and speaker, so I really have a lot to live up to in order that I might keep them impressed. One day we were having an in-depth discussion about the happenings of our day: the economic woes and different things our families seemed to be facing. It was for us a down day.

So, I began to wax eloquently, "Yes, sometimes in difficult times, we just have to pull ourselves up by the boot strings and make up our minds that everything is going to be all right." A silence followed my statement, and then as you can imagine, laughter erupted.

☙ Are You a Joy Maker?

"What?" I asked in confusion.

"Did you say boot strings?" My friend Phyllis asked.

Realizing my mistake, I quickly answered, "Well, life is so hard these days that we no longer have straps, but only strings to pull ourselves up with."

Isn't that pitiful? Not much joy around me that day, that's for sure. As you may surmise, they didn't fall for my quick response. But there are going to be times in your life when you feel like you really do only have strings to pull yourself up with. But be of good cheer, your Kodak moment is coming.

I so enjoy receiving tidbits via email. As is often the case, no one was given the proper credit for the random remarks. However, these tips on life brought a chuckle to my day, and made me be of good cheer. The email read: *Here are some great ways of dealing with the burdens of life:*

> *Accept that some days you're the pigeon, and some days you are the statue.*
>
> *Always keep your words soft and sweet, just in case you have to eat them.*
>
> *Drive carefully. It's not only cars that can be recalled by their maker.*
>
> *If you can't be kind, at least have the decency to be vague.*
>
> *It may be that your sole purpose in life is simply to serve as a warning to others.*

A Kodak Moment

Never put both feet in your mouth at the same time because then you won't have a leg to stand on.

Since it's the early worm that gets eaten by the bird, sleep late.

The second mouse gets the cheese.

When everything's coming your way, perhaps you're in the wrong lane.

Birthdays are good for you. The more you have, the longer you live.

Some mistakes are too much fun to only make once.

A truly happy person is one who can enjoy the scenery on a detour.

Most of my days do indeed consist of some kind of detour. But on the days when everything does not turn out as I planned, I hope I can enjoy the scenery on my unscheduled detour. And along the detour route, I want to look for the good in my rather unexpected situation. On the days that it is not so good, remember that it will get better. On those days, you will have to seek to find the joy.

Doctors say that a person can live without food for forty days, without sleep for twelve days, without water for six days, and without oxygen for five minutes. But it is impossible for a person to survive without hope. Life isn't always easy, but we must never lose our hope.

☜ Are You a Joy Maker?

Keep hoping for that Kodak moment. And if perhaps the picture of your life is not exactly what you thought it would be, if it is not that perfect Kodak moment, adjust the lens on your camera a bit and work with what you have to make the picture as beautiful as possible.

*My nephew,
Geoff Christian,
enjoying a Kodak moment*

Life may not be the party we hoped for, but while we're here, we should dance.
—Unknown

Life isn't a matter of milestones, but moments.
—Rose Kennedy

If you treat every situation as a life-and-death matter, you'll die a lot of times.
—Dean Smith

Interlude 2

Are You in the Picture?

The annual Christmas party is a time of enjoyment for our offices. We all look forward to spending our lunch hour together, eating delicious food, and receiving our Christmas gift. Soft Christmas music plays in the background, and tinkling glass and comfortable chatter are all elements of this event. "How much better could it get?" I thought, savoring the festive atmosphere at a recent party.

As we were indeed taking advantage of this momentous occasion, an unknown lady entered our midst and quickly hurried to the head table. She leaned over and spoke to General Superintendent Kenneth Haney, and he rose and left the room. Everyone looked up at his exit but resumed eating and fellowshipping. Within minutes he returned, and much to our surprise, he escorted the governor of the state of Missouri into our presence. We were taken aback at this unexpected visitor and stood to our feet and began to applaud. Governor Blunt acknowledged our accolades in a kindly manner and spent a few minutes thanking us for our prayers and support. We were somewhat awed by his unplanned appearance, but a few recovered enough to snap pictures. Governor Blunt was scheduled to be at a fundraiser next door to our room and decided to stop in and wish us a Merry Christmas. This surprising guest appearance was the talk of the afternoon.

Since my boss, General Secretary Jerry Jones, had allowed me to secure the location for our Christmas luncheon, I teasingly told everyone that I had scheduled this secret meeting just for their benefit. I continued to bring up the subject at every opportunity the rest of the afternoon whenever someone mentioned how neat it was that he took the time to stop by our meeting. Of course, since I enjoy doling out the orneriness, I do get my share of teasing back in return.

Later that afternoon I received an email from my co-worker, Diana Dunlap, with the subject, "I've Hit the Big Time." I quickly clicked on the attached picture and found an image of Governor Blunt standing next to Brother Haney, and much to my dismay, my supposed friend Diana standing serenely there in the picture, smiling Mona-Lisa-style right at Governor Blunt. Let me add a bit of insight to this situation. I had saved Diana a chair since she was running late and had initially sat in that chair. When she arrived,

Are You in the Picture?

I switched to the next chair to make it easier for her to slip in unobserved. Thus, because of my decision, I was completely out of the picture. So close to being in the picture, and yet so far away.

I'm sure you have most likely encountered instances just like the one I mentioned above. Although I am facetious about missing out on being in the picture, in the journey of life it often seems like we are always at the wrong place at the right time or the right place at the wrong time. You know what I mean. Why is the line you get in always the slowest? Why is your server usually the one who ignores your efforts to gain her attention? Why is that fabulous sale product no longer available? Oh, such trials we face as we meander through the corridors of time, trying our best to do right, to live right, and help those in need. Why do things never turn out the way we planned? Woe to me. Poor little old me. Negativism is my middle name. And the way things are going, it could become my last name.

Yes, life is not always fair. And perhaps you have a person in your life like my husband, who when I complain softly reminds me that we are not promised fairness, only grace to deal with what happens to us. "Okay, okay," I think, trying to keep a right spirit in spite of my frustration. But as the Bible so ably instructs me, "Wives submit yourselves to your husband." And so I humbly submit. (I hope he's not reading this!)

༄ Are You a Joy Maker?

It seems there is much to complain about. However, perhaps we should look to Australia for some answers to this query. A sign was seen in one of their shop windows that read, "Yesterday was the deadline for all complaints." Okay, then. It makes one think, that's for certain.

I think of the saying I heard once as a child that said, "I complained of the pain in my leg, until I saw a man with no legs, and decided, I did not have it bad at all." My mother once told me that when you think things are bad, look around and you will find someone worse off than you. Then you can count your blessings like you should.

When we look at the big picture of life, we might be surprised at what we see. One thing we most likely will see is that we are usually not front and center, stealing the limelight from everyone else. But that is not what the big picture is really about anyway. The big picture is about putting God first in your life, then others, and then yourself. In Mark 12:30, it says, "And thou shalt love the Lord thy God with all thy heart, and with all thy soul, and with all thy mind, and with all thy strength: this is the first commandment." If we can grasp this picture, perhaps we would most likely appear in more pictures than we could possibly imagine. We could be a part of more Kodak moments than we thought possible.

So I may not appear in any pictures standing next to the governor like my wonderful friend Diana,

Are You in the Picture?

but I will appear with Him in the sky and forever be with Him. And when we see Him, who will care about any old picture anyway?

Governor Matt Blunt and Kenneth Haney with my friend, Diana Dunlap

You only live once—but if you work it right, once is enough.
—Joe E. Lewis

Are You a Joy Maker?

Enjoying time with Sister Pugh and Pam and Breanna Pugh

A joyful hug from Kara

Interlude 3

Making the Right Choice

My iron-poor blood just could not seem to get going one fine morning. I had returned quite late the night before from a trip with my husband and had to arise early to go to work, and I was not in the best of the spirits. I quickly clothed myself and made an endeavor to be in my right mind. Hurrying down the stairs, I unfortunately remembered that I had forgotten to take my thyroid medication, which was upstairs, and which I definitely knew I would need that day. So, I dashed back into the bathroom and gulped down that important little pill.

On my way to work, I began to feel a bit funny. I had difficulty focusing and felt very tired. I could not believe how very tired I felt. I hoped that getting to work would help invigorate my constitution. However, when I arrived at work, I felt like doing nothing but falling asleep. My wonderful friends began to gather around, expressing their gladness to see me back, and I could barely figure out who was talking to me. Now becoming quite concerned, I stepped into a side office and sat down to try to get myself together. Thinking a piece of gum might rally my spirits, I began shuffling through the things in my purse, and much to my chagrin, found my thyroid pills. Then I realized why I was feeling out of sorts.

The night before I sat my medication in the bathroom. Now, I am not a pill popper. I take a maintenance pill to counteract migraines, thyroid medication, and then I have a strong medication I have to take occasionally for severe headaches. And yes, you guessed it. I inadvertently took that knockout pill instead of the thyroid medication. I mean after all, they are the same color and are similar in size. My time was limited and I didn't have time to find my glasses. I had to make a quick choice. Unfortunately, it was not the right choice. Thus, I spent a rather miserable day trying to appear as if I was my normal self when I was anything but that.

Life is full of choices. Every day we make choices. What we choose to wear, what we choose to eat, what we choose to do, etc. Choices, choices.

I have often wondered at the awesomeness of God. He gave us the right to choose what we will do with our lives. He had the power to make us serve Him, but He loved us so much that He wanted us to choose to serve Him.

Making the Right Choice

There are many in the Scriptures who made the right choice. One in particular I enjoy reading about is Joshua. When the whole camp of Israel seemed to turn from God, he stood strong and became a leader in their midst. Joshua 24:15 explains well the stalwart nature of the man: "And if it seem evil unto you to serve the Lord, choose you this day whom ye will serve, whether the gods which your fathers served that were on the other side of the flood, or the gods of the Amorites, in whose land ye dwell; but as for me and my house, we will serve the Lord."

Joshua made a choice that even if no one else chose to serve the Lord, he and his family (or house) would. He took a stand and made the right choice. Thus, because of his choice, he influenced the land of Israel. Joshua 24:24 says, "And the people said unto Joshua, The Lord our God will we serve, and his voice will we obey." And they continued to serve the Lord as indicated by Joshua 24:31: "And Israel served the Lord all the days of Joshua, and all the days of the elders, that overlived Joshua, and which had known all the works of the Lord, that he had done for Israel." Because of the strong choice Joshua made, he left an inheritance and legacy that lived long in the nation of Israel.

Pride and Prejudice is a favorite book of mine. I enjoy reading the verbiage of its author, Jane Austin. One line that particularly caught my attention in the book was when the older sister Jane was trying to recover from a broken heart. The man of her dreams had left without any explanation or reason. She believed him to be in love with her and suddenly learned he had left. Jane and Elizabeth Bennett were in the garden conversing. Elizabeth was trying to encourage her sister and told her she did not like to see her unhappy. Jane responded, "I am resolved to think of him no more. Truly, Lizzie, I promise I shall be well. I shall be myself again. I shall be perfectly content."[1] Sometimes we have to give ourselves a pep talk like that. We have to lift ourselves up and talk ourselves into accepting an uneasy situation. Jane chose to be content in spite of what seemed a hopeless situation. She made the right choice.

Philippians 4:11 says, "Not that I speak in respect of want, for I have learned, in whatsoever state I am, therewith to be content."

My husband is a minister, and we have moved several times since we have been married. He was talking to me at one point about moving to take a pastorate in North Carolina. He asked, "So how would you feel about that?" I responded with that verse in Philippians. However, with much impertinence, I added, "So whatsoever state I am in, therewith I will be content." Needless to say, he was not much impressed with my words of wisdom. He slowly grinned and shook his head with tolerance,

Making the Right Choice

which he has seemed to do quite often since we have been married.

We sometimes have to make up our mind that no matter what happens to us, we will be happy. We have to make the choice to rejoice. And it may mean making some effort to be joyful. We have to become joy makers ourselves. As with my family, I sometimes have to be the joy maker for my girls. And in turn, they become joy makers for me when I need it as well. I think it turns out quite well all the way around, even if I say so myself.

So, if there are times in life when you don't really want to do something, but feel it is of utmost necessity, make the right choice. Be happy anyway.

http://howardhuge.com
(Used by permission)

◯ Are You a Joy Maker?

We act as though comfort and luxury were the chief requirements of life, when all that we need to make us really happy is something to be enthusiastic about.
—Charles Kingsley

Get rich quick! Count your blessings!
—Unknown

---

[1] *http://www.script-o-rama.com//p/pride-and-prejudice-script-transcript.html*

Interlude 4

Not My Day

I worked diligently to pry my right eye open so that I could venture a glance at my most dependable radio clock. Enjoying a few more moments to enjoy the warmth of my soft bed on this cold winter morning, I had plenty of time as the radio station hadn't as yet played the National Anthem. I mean, after all, just like clockwork, they played various versions of our adored anthem at 6:00 am without fail. So I decided to close my eyes and rest a few more minutes until I heard the familiar music.

Alas, to my shock and amazement, the time suddenly glared threateningly at me. "6:30" it accused. "What in the world are you doing laying there as if you had not a care in the world?" Oh, my word! Here I was nestled all snug in my bed, while visions of sugar plums danced in my head! When right in my head there arose such a clatter, I sprang from the bed

☜ Are You a Joy Maker?

remembering Kalee had to be at school at quite an early hour.

So my day did not start off in a calm and peaceful manner, even though it was the Christmas season. And unfortunately, it continued in that mode. I hurried on to work and rushed in the door, only to find that I had left my phone plugged in back in the car. Although I had just taken off my coat, I put it back on and trekked out to the SUV because there is absolutely no way I can be without my cell phone. I mean, after all, I might get the urge to text since I am quite proficient at it.

I finally arrived back inside and tried to get my desk in order, feeling somewhat like Hezekiah might have when he received his dire message. I worked diligently, trying to answer numerous calls and was so intent and dedicated to the job I almost forgot a doctor's appointment that had been scheduled for some time. Again, I dashed for the door and hurried to another part of town. Not feeling my best, and most likely not looking my best, I shuffled quickly into the door, not indicating that anyone else was present in the room, signed in, and had just sat down to catch my breath when they called my name. Now, how often does that happen? I mean, I can arrive at a doctor's office thirty minutes early and still sit another hour before they ever call my name. And just when I need a little reprieve, they are ready for me to "come on back." Unbelievable.

Not My Day

Finished with the appointment, I backed out and ran over the curb. Taking a quick look around, I was quite relieved to see that no one was watching my inept driving skills. I hurried back to the office because I wanted to get back in time to go to chapel as I definitely needed to pray today. Finally, some good news. After prayer, I did feel a bit better.

My hubby called me to go to lunch, and because he is always running late anyway, I took my good easy time and decided to finish up a few things. I sauntered down the stairs and there he stood, waiting patiently for me. Again, another unexpected turn of events.

A busy afternoon followed the hectic morning, and so to rejuvenate me and my wonderful coworkers, I volunteered to go get us all Diet Cokes at the McDonald's down the road. My suggestion was met with much anticipation, so I donned my coat and . . . could not find my car keys. I looked and looked. I went to hubby's office, but no, he did not have them. I came back to my desk, had all the coworkers looking for them, and even checked all the restrooms, checked with the receptionist, but to no avail. I then went to borrow my husband's car so I wouldn't waste any more time and scurried out the door.

I pulled up to McDonald's and waited patiently for the attendant to take my order. I had difficulty understanding her, but went ahead and ordered four large Diet Cokes. With muffled, non-recognizable words, she answered me, and I simply said "thanks" and pulled up to the window. While pulling out my billfold, I noticed a small, very small, pocket in my purse. And guess what was in that obscure pocket? You guessed it! I'm sorry that this is not a game in which you win money because the answer was so difficult. Yes, my keys. How silly I felt! I had nearly all of the office looking for them and they were right in my purse the whole time. Now, how would I explain that without looking totally ridiculous?

Because of my great discovery, I had not paid attention when the lady swiped my card, so when she handed me one medium Diet Coke, I looked startled. I told her that I ordered four large Diet Cokes, and she acted like I had lost my senses. Well, perhaps I had. Who knows? The way my day had gone, I might have ordered one medium instead of four larges. Anyway, she adjusted the order, not very kindly, and I journeyed back to the office.

Trying to open the door with my large beverages intact, I dropped the straws and had to call for back up to retrieve them. Alas, I arrived safely bearing the magnanimous gifts for my coworkers. That was just a brief synopsis, and since this chapter is becoming quite lengthy, I best stop there and not share the further trials that came my way.

Since it was Christmas, my favorite time of the year, I decided to adjust a well-known Christmas reading to accommodate my peril.

Not My Day

THE NIGHT BEFORE "NOT MY DAY"

'Twas the night before Not My Day, when all through the house
Not a creature was stirring, not even a mouse;
The chosen clothes were all hung in the closet with care,
In hopes that a fast and easy exit soon would be there;
The daughters, hubby, and me, of course, were nestled all snug in our beds,
While visions of a McDonald's parfait danced in my head;
Of course, I didn't have on a 'kerchief,
And the hubby definitely did not have on a cap,
We were simply waiting for our much dreaded alarm to resound.
When a startled glance at the clock made me arise with such a clatter,
I sprang from the bed to see if Kalee was already beginning her incessant chatter.
Away to the window I flew like a flash,
Tore open the shutters and threw up the sash.
Of course, much to my disappointment, there was no new-fallen snow

❧ Are You a Joy Maker?

All that I could see were the clouds and fog below
And that was all that my wondering eyes could find to appear,
So because Kalee had to be early at school or else experience severe fear,
I became a little old driver, so lively and quick,
And I knew in a moment we were going to have to have a Starbuck's fix.
More rapid than eagles with purses we came,
And we whistled, and shouted, and called our favorite drinks by name.
"Now, Latte! now, Mocha! Espresso and such!
Come on, I so much want a grande drink, but need something skinny and tall instead!
Through the top of their window! Right straight through their wall!
We grabbed our drinks and dashed away all!"

Now, I know that you thoroughly enjoyed that repertoire. But at least it gave you a better insight into a "not my day."

Feeling grumpy and a bit put out, I started a "poor pitiful" party. But perhaps that short prayer meeting I had earlier in the day kicked in because as I was trying to scrounge up some good reason to be upset, I took a minute to think back. Perhaps I was not the only one having a "not my day." My little Kalee was definitely having a "not my day" because I did not wake her up in time to get things together like she normally did, so I'm certain her day did not go as well.

And the lady at the doctor's office. Instead of me being thankful I got in early, did I look frustrated at her and cause her day to change? Instead of smiling at my husband for being there, I made some sarcastic comment about "Well, you're here for once." Did I make him have a "not my day." And was my frustration obvious to the little lady at the drive through window and make her have a "not my day." Looking back, I feel sad that I might have influenced so many people to have a "not my day." Dear me. I think I need to pray again.

So, I am certain you have experienced a "not my day" at some point. Unfortunately, we are all human and we do make mistakes. But I want to do a better job at being sensitive to the needs of those around me. I don't want to judge because I might have been delayed in receiving something I wanted, like my Diet Coke. Now, giving myself the benefit of the doubt, I wasn't downright mean to anyone, but I wasn't downright nice either. I do know that I can work on doing a better job of reaching out to those around us. I want people to say "Wow, that was one nice lady" when I walk away, instead of saying, "I wonder who she thinks she is." Which impression

◌ Are You a Joy Maker?

would most influence someone to approach you about Jesus? No, you don't have to answer that. We all know the answer.

Several years ago, when my husband Mark and I were pastoring a home missions church, he picked me up for my lunch break from the law firm at which I was employed. We went to one of my favorite restaurants, and I was not at my best. I was four months pregnant and nauseated. I needed food, and you know how we can get sometimes when we need food. Our server was a young lady who just didn't seem to have it together. I couldn't get her to bring me any bread, and she was so slow bringing our drinks. I was fussing and complaining to Mark, and he quietly said, "Babe, just be patient. She's probably doing her very best."

"But I'm hungry here," I answered. "And if I don't get something now, I may just throw up right here."

About that time, she came back to our table and finally brought some bread and our drinks. I took just long enough to catch a glimpse of the young lady's face, and it was filled with anxiety. Her eyes looked so very tired and she softly said, "Please forgive me for being so slow today. I just can't get my mind on things."

"Oh, that's all right," Mark answered.

"No, it's really not," she answered. "I'm just having a few difficulties right now."

"Oh?" my husband queried. "I'm sorry to hear that."

Then she started talking. "Yes, my nine-month baby is in intensive care and they can't figure out what's wrong with her." She quickly wiped away a tear. "I wanted to stay with her today, but we so much need the money that I couldn't afford to be off work. So, I'm not doing a very good job."

Talk about feeling like a jerk. I would have been the first to raise my hand. Mark told her we would pray for her and, in fact, he had the chance to pray for the baby at the hospital. Because of my husband's sensitivity, we had the chance to reach out to that young lady in need. We helped her when she was having a "not my day." Well, my husband did anyway. I couldn't take credit for it because I was so wrapped up in my own "not my day."

How did He handle what could have been seen by the grandstands of time and eternity as a "not my day"? It would hardly seem anyone would want to make this kind of day their own. It was not like He, the Savior of the world, really had wanted the conditions to be this way. But He had determined long before that whatever was needed to correct the complexities and mounting chaos of sin He would consider as HIS own burden to solve. What kind of love makes a moment like that His day? To the disciples, He stated, "Mine hour is not yet come" (John 2:4).

◈ Are You a Joy Maker?

He allowed Himself to be taken from a garden in the midst of prayer before a governor who knew only minimal facts about him. To Pilate, His response was clear, "To this end was I born and for this cause came I into the world" (John 18:37). He was beaten severely and then forced in His weakened condition to carry a huge cross through the crowd of people that continued to taunt Him and scream vicious curse words at Him. Then before a multitude and His beloved mother, He was crucified. He suffered the most violent execution known in that day and time. Yet, in excruciating pain beyond description, He reached out to a low-life thief dying on the cross next to Him. This scourge of society was granted forgiveness by the Savior of the World: "Today shalt thou be with me in paradise" (Luke 23:43). What miraculous love He showed on His "not my day!"

So, when you are having a "not my day," make an effort to become a joy maker. Remember how much Jesus gave when He had the worst day anyone could ever have experienced, and yet He willingly gave His life so that we might live.

The story of the ages tells us all again that in life we have a Friend who is willing to take all the "not my days" we may have and carry them for us. His mission was clear. If the "not my day" is bigger than you can handle, you have a Friend who will not only help you, but will take you through it.

Not My Day

*My sweet little daughter,
Courtney, having a
"Not My Day."*

There is no such thing in anyone's life as an unimportant day.
—Alexander Woollcott

∽ Are You a Joy Maker?

With childhood friend, Renee Flowers

Kalee and Courtney sharing joyful smiles

Interlude 5

Life Is Just Not Fair

I'm feeling a bit sorry for myself at the moment. I found out that I have pneumonia again, and I have coughed and coughed my head off. My family has gone to a Youth Congress, and although I don't begrudge them (really!) their fun, I still feel a bit blue. In my solitude, I came across some memoirs I had written about my dad, and a few tears have entered the scene. And it's Thanksgiving Eve, and there is usually a lot more activity going on in my family. However, this Thanksgiving didn't quite turn out exactly the way I had planned.

Oh, now, don't get me wrong and become judgmental. Give me a chance to explain. I know how blessed I am and never hesitate to thank God for His merciful kindness to my life. But that doesn't take away the moments of disappointment that unexpectedly come my way. And as they say (whoever "they" are), when it rains, it pours. Several other major

∽ Are You a Joy Maker?

developments have happened in the last few weeks that seem somewhat overwhelming. And then this sickness thing popped up. Thus, I guess I'm just going through a little down time.

Seems like I'm not the only one who has felt downtrodden. Wasn't it David who asked why the wicked prospered? (See Psalm 73.) Oh, I so know what he meant. Here we are trying to live godly lives, and everything seems to be going awry, while those who seem to treat everything and everyone with disregard seem to have all kinds of things going their way.

For example, a dear friend related an incident that happened to them just a few days ago. Their credit card number was stolen, and thus the bank had to stop the use of the debit card. They had to wait about ten days for their new card to come in but finally, it arrived. She was sick, so her good husband ran a few errands for her and went to get some medicine. He also stopped by the ATM to get some cash with the new card. He drove away from the ATM and was not far down the road when he realized he had left his card in the ATM. Quickly hurrying back to the bank in hopes of retrieving the card, unfortunately he discovered the ATM's security measure had pulled the card inside. So, he again had lost his card. He arrived home, hungry from his escapade and fixed himself the perfect sandwich. Reaching around to grab something behind him, their dog grabbed the sandwich and gulped it down faster than a speeding bullet. Needless to say, the husband had reached his limit. He reprimanded the dog and put him outside for punishment. Thus, life had handed him some rather unfair advantages and to add fuel to the fire, he lost his dinner as well. Life is just not fair.

We are blessed to have a wonderful extended family. One family I think of in particular is our cousins, Donald and Robin Ruppanner. Donald is my husband's cousin, and I first became acquainted with him when Mark and I were dating. Mark traveled a great deal and was never around to escort me to various church functions. Donald worked in Amarillo where we lived, so he ended up going with my mom, dad, and me to various events. Donald and I became very good friends and we had a lot of fun together. Donald had a quiet demeanor, but he always had a ready laugh when I told some joke or shared various anecdotes with him. When Mark and I became engaged, I told Donald if it had been permissible, that I would have asked him to be my "Man of Honor."

God blessed Donald with a wonderful wife, Robin James, who was in fact a good friend of mine from youth camp days. What a bubbly, positive, happy, joyful person Robin is! She loves life and is one of the most caring people I have ever met. Donald and Robin have had to deal with some major difficulties in their lives. Their first precious child, James Stewart, was born with Down syndrome, and he brought so much

Are You a Joy Maker?

joy to everyone's life. But in the first year of his life, he was diagnosed with a very rare form of leukemia. Sadly, God took little James home. During this time, these two wonderful people stood strong and ended up encouraging everyone else around them.

A few years later they were blessed with another child, Austin. He also experienced some health problems, but thankfully God touched his life and he is now attending Texas A&M University. Only a few years after Austin was born, Robin was diagnosed with Multiple Sclerosis. We were all devastated by this unexpected news. It seemed so unfair that Robin had to endure this disease. She was the greatest person! Of course, Mrs. Positive again encouraged us all and told us that she was going to be just fine.

Then another tragedy struck our wonderful cousins. Robin's only sister, Gay, a wonderful friend of mine as well, was killed in an automobile accident along with her young son. We just could not believe it! Again, Robin and Donald stood strong through another storm. I could go on for some time about all the things that have happened to Donald and Robin. Donald lost his mom with an aneurysm and then his sister to breast cancer. Their lives have been touched with so much unfairness.

However, when my phone rings and I pick it up, I am amazed to hear Robin's lilting voice, "Hi, Karla. How are you?" Although she struggles with pain and numbness and all the other affects of MS, instead of talking about herself, she always wants to hear about me instead. Donald and Robin have not let the unfairness of life destroy them. They still serve God with all their might. They greet everyone with a smile and encourage and uplift those around them. When our daughter, Kara, got married, Donald and Robin stayed over and helped us get the final decorations out of the building on Saturday. And, yes, Robin worked along with the rest of us. She would pile flowers onto her lap and motor in her skooter chair out to the car. When I cautioned her about taking it easy, she promptly replied, "Oh, this is fun. I love helping." Robin is a joy maker.

So when I get to feeling sorry for myself and thinking I have it bad, I think of Donald and Robin. I have never heard them even make the statement "Life is not fair." Instead I hear, "We're doing great. God is so good to us. We are so blessed." It comes down to our attitude. It is all in how we handle what comes our way during this journey through life.

So a marching band may not be playing an opening theme for your grand entrance. Or a symphony may not ever play a piece of music written entirely in your honor. You may never personally meet a king or president. But just remember you have met someone who cares for you beyond what you could possibly imagine. Jesus, the Savior of the world, knows your name, and that is the most important thing of all.

∞ Are You a Joy Maker?

Everything else pales in comparison to His touch on our lives. If your life seems unfair, I give you Jesus.

If the ship of your life,
Is tossing on the sea of strife,
You need someone.
And if it seems you're all alone
And your house is not a home,
You need someone.
If you feel life isn't fair
There's no one left to share
All those lonely days and nights
When things just don't turn out right

And you want someone to care
Someone to just be there.
You need someone.

I give you Jesus,
He's the peace that passeth all understanding
I give you Jesus,
He's that perfect love that casteth out all fear,
I give you Jesus
He's the water that you drink and never thirst again,
I give you Jesus, my friend,
I Give You Jesus!

Words by Becky Fender
(Used by permission)

Life Is Just Not Fair ༶

Robin Ruppanner and me

Are You a Joy Maker?

Laughing with friends Carol Johns and Phyllis Jones

Kara and hubby, Bobby McCool, spreading Christmas joy

Interlude 6

The Natural Thing to Do

Our family enjoys going out to eat. With our busy schedules, it just seems more work than necessary to plan meals and meet the schedules of five different people. There are more occasions than I care to remember of times when I have prepared a meal for the family, doing as I supposed a good mother should, only to find that two or more of the children had previous plans that came up unannounced that they just could not avoid missing. Thus, my picturesque dream of our family gathering for a lovely prepared dinner around a lavishly laid table with the fireplace blazing in the background and our laughing faces exhibiting our joy of just being together never seemed to happen. Hence, eating out was usually our chosen plan of action.

I have encouraged the girls to be conservative when it comes to spending money. How well I did in my endeavor has not yet been revealed. But, since we did spend several meals eating out at a restaurant, I became quite adept at saving the almighty dollar. When they were very young, I found out what restaurants offered kids a free meal and we frequented those hot spots. I had it down to an art, so much so that I knew the specific restaurant that offered free meals for children most every night of the week. Thus, we usually only had to pay for a full meal ticket only once a week.

I suppose we were fortunate to have little girls because they were not big eaters. Now I trust you don't judge me harshly here, but my two girls could split a kid's meal and be perfectly full. No, they did not starve. They just didn't eat very much. Then when our third daughter began to eat regular food, they could all order one regular meal and split it. The only problem we ever encountered is diplomatically trying to get the three to agree on one specific meal. On the whole, our arrangement worked well for us for a long time.

Because of my effectual efforts of being frugal, our friends often tease me about our "splitting" efforts. However, I have learned to bear the burden and looked to the Word of God for guidance. John 16:33 says, "In the world ye shall have tribulation: but be of good cheer; I have overcome the world." So in spite of the abuse I suffer, I continue to be of good cheer.

A few years back, my friend Phyllis Jones came by to see me during one of my "not so good"

The Natural Thing to Do ∞

headache days. She kindly suggested taking the girls to eat so I would have one less worry. Of course, the girls loved to go with "Aunt Phyllis" if they ever got the opportunity. They went to a restaurant and just after they were seated, she looked at the three and said, "Tonight there will be no splitting. Everyone gets their own plate." The girls, thankfully showing the good manners I had attempted to instill in them, expressed their reticence, but Aunt Phyllis insisted and would not take "no" for an answer. Thus, they were all bought their own plates and still to this day talk about that night. If nothing else was accomplished on that evening, at least Phyllis now understood why the girls always split their meals. She had to ask for to-go boxes that were piled high with their uneaten food. The girls were able to eat for almost a week on all they brought home! (Not quite, but sometimes one feels the need to speak evangelistically.) To this day, the girls continue to split their meals. It just seems the natural thing to do.

For something to become natural, it takes some training. Training involves doing something repetitively until a person finds it easy or natural to perform a task. It is the process of teaching to learn a skill or job. Confession time: I remember as a teenager looking in the mirror and trying to find my best smile. I practiced smiling. Now, times have changed somewhat. My girls still practice smiling as well, but in a different manner. They use their handy

∽ Are You a Joy Maker?

digital camera or their cell phone cameras to capture that perfect smile, and they can delete the smiles they don't like. Times have really changed. I never got to review my smiles to see which one was the best. I had to use my memory log and hope I chose the right one.

A smile is silent, but can turn into a noise of jubilation and joy. If perhaps you aren't used to smiling, try practicing to smile. Oh, you may not feel comfortable looking in a mirror or taking pictures of your smile, but just try smiling at that person at the post office, or at the grocery store, or at the mall. In no time at it, it will become natural for you to smile at everyone you meet. And I can almost guarantee they will return a smile to you as well.

Smiling can lead to laughter. Laughter can be a side effect of a smile. I so enjoy hearing the commercials for certain medications when after telling what they can do for you, in rapid speech, they list the side effects, which usually are not good. They sound so dire! But I can assure you beyond a shadow of a doubt that laughter is a good side effect of a smile. Laughter begins with a smile.

I've been told that it is easy to make me laugh, and I'm not always certain if that is a compliment or a complaint. I do know that my girls say it is easy to find me in a crowd by my laughter. I also am not certain if that is a compliment or complaint. But I will take it as a compliment because what better way to know a person than by his or her laughter. Perhaps there should be a Scripture that says, "You shall know them by their laughter."

While writing this chapter, I can hear the laughter of some dear friends. One in particular is Carol Johns. How I love being around my wonderful friend! She is full of joy and laughter. Laughter comes easy to her. I once spoke at a ladies' breakfast and being nervous, I asked Carol to sit close to the front so I could hear her laughter as my encouragement. I knew if no one else laughed at my jokes, she would because she always had. Laughter was a natural thing for her do.

Unfortunately, there are times of non-laughter, especially in our families. Perhaps there are times we may feel like the little boy I remember hearing about in one of our Sunday school classes. The students were asked to locate verses that related to their families. The teacher asked, "So what verse comes to mind when you think of your brothers or sisters?" One little guy raised his hand and answered, "Thou shalt not kill." Not the answer perhaps the teacher was seeking, but a statement that more than explains the frustration that may at times come to our homes.

When Kalee was very young, she used to get so frustrated when she was trying to learn something new or when she realized she could not go with her older sisters somewhere. I found that teasing her

☙ Are You a Joy Maker?

and laughing with her always restored her good humor. She was easily cajoled. It still seems to work with her now. When a tough situation arises, looking at the positive aspects and finding something to joke and laugh about helps ease the tension in her life. Yes, the Christian women do tend to be over-emotional, and we would be the first to admit it. But we also are the first to find something to laugh about as well. We do love to laugh!

One thing I desire to have more of in my family is an apparent sign of joy and laughter. I hope our home will have much laughter and that laughter becomes a natural part of our daily regimen. There is so much junk out in the cold world that our homes should be a haven from all that muck and mire. I want my children to desire to come home, not trying to find any place to go *but* home. I feel strongly that making your home joyful and full of laughter is the key to bringing them home.

Is laughter a natural thing for you to do? Is joy easy to access in your home? If not, perhaps a little training might help. When those difficult times come, try smiling. And then try laughing. Oh, it may not erupt immediately. It may start out as only a chortle. But I have so often heard the statement, "It's better to laugh than to cry." So if laughter is not the normal part of your day, perhaps you can start training now. It won't be long until laughter is a natural thing for you to do.

The Natural Thing to Do ෆ

Phyllis Jones and I

ෆෆෆෆෆෆෆෆ

If you're not using your smile, you're like a man with a million dollars in the bank and no checkbook.
—Les Giblin

Sometimes your joy is the source of your smile, but sometimes your smile can be the source of your joy.
—Thich Nhat Hanh

We shall never know all the good that a simple smile can do.
—Mother Teresa

∽ Are You a Joy Maker?

Having fun with Olga Hyde and Phyllis Jones

One and only son-in-law, Bobby, with Kalee and Courtney

Interlude 7

Making History

The phone rang and I knew the call we had dreaded to receive had come. Tensing my muscles, I listened as my husband answered and then turned to me and said, "I'm so sorry." Tears filled my eyes as I knew my wonderful dad had passed on to his reward. It was hard to imagine life without him. He brought such joy to our family.

Dad always had a funny story or joke to tell. My sister and I loved to listen to him tell about things that happened in different church services, which he would share on occasion with us. He had a wealth of such stories! He told of one such service when the Spirit was moving, and one man, responding to the move of God, testified, "I feel so humble I feel like just going behind that door." A lady in the congregation quickly stood and said, "I feel so humble too, I think I'll go behind the door with Brother Smith."

◯ Are You a Joy Maker?

Dad had a lot of famous sayings and quips. One he often used was "Just hold my leg up in prayer." He tells the story of a lady who once requested prayer for a friend who had broken her leg. She requested prayer by saying, "I think we need to hold Sister So and So's leg up in prayer." Every time Dad would feel a bit under the weather (another one of his sayings), he would say, "Perhaps if you would just hold my leg up in prayer."

He once named a street in our town Snuff Street. Being a child, I just took it for granted that the street was really named that. When I got older, he laughed while hearing me try to give directions to someone by saying, "You go down Snuff Street." He quickly explained that he called it that only because he was frustrated with all the dips in the road. He said, "You go a block and take a dip."

"Ignorance gone to seed" was a quip he often used when it seemed someone didn't understand as quickly as he thought they should have. He, of course, did not say that in front of the person. He only said it when we were in private conversation.

Dad was a kind man and cared about so many people. However, he was a quite a prankster and a joker as well. When Elder William Dean moved his family to Friona, he and Dad became fast friends. Often they would play practical jokes on each other. There was an elderly woman in the church in Clovis, New Mexico, who often called Dad and just wanted to chat about some situation in the section. He would try to be patient with her, but he expressed his frustration of her continual phone calls to Brother Dean. She would always begin her conversation in a rather whiney voice with "Brother Jim Bob . . . ." On one such occasion, the phone rang. As he answered, he heard the voice of whom he thought was Brother Dean playing a joke. "Brother Jim Bob . . ." it began. Thinking he would catch Brother Dean at his own game, he answered in the same trembling voice, "Whatey?" He was so mortified when he realized it really was the dear saint from Clovis. He fumbled a bit for words but quickly covered his mistake with kind words and concern for her health.

Dad loved picking on us all. He often told my Aunt Doris when she was a little girl that she must have been vaccinated by a phonograph needle as she just wouldn't be quiet. When he and Mom were dating, he offered Aunt Doris fifty cents just to be quiet for thirty minutes. My offer was much lower, usually around five cents. I should have negotiated for more funds. My Aunt Doris did get the upper hand on him many times as she must certainly have needed the money to be quiet that long.

Dad was quite a snappy dresser. He enjoyed looking stylish. Joe, my brother-in-law, made the comment, "He was the only man I know who could wear white shoes, a double-breasted blue blazer, and a bowtie and still pull it off."

∽ Are You a Joy Maker?

My dad loved helping with anything he could at church. When he and Mom retired, they moved to Austin, Texas, to be closer to my sister. He was thrilled to be able to manage their bookstore. Often Geoff, my nephew, would stop by the bookstore to say hi to Papaw. Papaw would look up with his quick smile and say, "Now who are you again?"

His joking manner did not stop even in his time of sickness. Once when Mom became irritated with him because he didn't seem to hear what she was saying, he answered, "I can hear. I'm not a crazy man."

I flew down to see Dad during one of his difficult times. I am so thankful I had those few days with him. I was sitting by his hospital bed, and again Mom said something to him and he didn't respond. "Jim Bob," she said rather loudly, "Do you want me to get you something from downstairs?" He answered her and after she left, he leaned over in a rather conspiratorial tone and said to me, "She thinks I can't hear her, but I can."

Dad lived life conservatively, and I can credit him for teaching me to do the same. Dad and Mom both worked diligently to make certain they were as frugal as possible. Joe, my brother-in-law, often tells of the Saturday shopping trip he took with Dad. Thinking he was going only to the grocery store, he ended up being gone for several hours as Papaw visited various places where the candy was cheaper at one place, several other items at a grocery store that offered coupons, and finally traveling several miles further to a place that had the best price on gas. If he could save any money, he would go the extra mile to do so.

Dad loved going to the grocery store and bringing home lots of candy, cokes, etc. My sister Vicki and I remember that we never seemed to run out of drinks as he made certain of that. He didn't mind running errands for us, which I thought was quite something. One Saturday, Mom and I asked him to run a few more errands than usual. Good-naturedly, he answered, "Sometimes I feel like I'm the Holy Ghost. I'm only an errand boy."

Dad also loved cooking. On Saturday mornings when we would visit after we left home, pots and pans would begin banging quite early, and then a booming voice would resound down the hall, "Breakfast is served in the diner. Come and get it before it gets cold." And we would drag out of bed to see a table full of biscuits, gravy, eggs, sausage, and bacon—the works.

He loved working crossword puzzles. When he finally retired, one of his daily routines would be to get the paper and immediately locate the puzzle. He often made the comment, "I've got to get my homework done."

And Papaw enjoyed helping the kids as well with their homework or whatever. Our middle daughter Courtney was struggling with learning her multiplication tables in the second grade, and while Mark and I were gone on a trip, he worked with her that whole week until she made 100 percent on her tests. My little cousin McKenna would stack a pile of books up when she knew Mom and Dad were coming to visit because she knew Uncle Papaw would read to her.

Dad went out of his way for children on so many occasions. My parents were fortunate to have Rex Johnson as their pastor. At Dad's funeral service, Pastor "J" (as Dad referred to him) told about his little grandson always going in the bookstore for candy. He noticed one time that Kaden only had a quarter and did not have enough money to purchase his favorite Momentos candy. Miraculously, the Momentos just happened to be on sale that day. He said he watched as the little guy left the store with a smile on his face with his prized purchase. Pastor Johnson was certain that Dad covered the loss.

Yes, Dad was a caring man. He loved the church in Texico, New Mexico, and worked so hard to make it a success. Dad could have easily been called the Praise Leader of the 1950s, '60s, and '70s. He was leading choruses before anyone knew what a praise leader was. He always seemed to find just the right song to sing at just the right time and would sing with such sincerity and praise that it would move the crowd to worship as well. He loved the Lord and served Him with everything in him.

Understanding God's Word

He was not only the piano player, a Sunday school teacher, the church secretary, and often head of fundraising efforts, but he would also clean the church on Saturday as well. He would coax Vicki and me to come along and help. When I wanted to vacuum or do some more important job, he would tell me how important it was to pick up all the papers and Kleenexes that were left in the book holders on the back of the pews. Before we could go to Clovis, New Mexico, to shop, we first had to clean the church.

Often Mom and Dad would come keep our girls when Mark and I had to go on overseas trips. On one such occasion, Dad pulled out, not seeing an oncoming car. Kara and Courtney yelled, "Papaw, hurry! There's a car coming." Trying to get out of the way of the oncoming car, they hit a huge pothole. "Merciful God!" he said, more in frustration than in prayer. "Papaw!" the girls scolded. Realizing his mistake, he quickly added, "Well, He is merciful, isn't He?"

And God was indeed merciful to my dad. During difficult situations, Dad always led his family in trusting God.

Dad made history, perhaps not in the best-known history books of the land, but with his family, his friends, and his church. We watched as he lived his life with unselfish candor. He gave of himself in all aspects of his life. And he taught us how to live life with joy and happiness. Dad always had humor to share and found something positive in life's situations. What a legacy for us to follow!

One such lady comes to mind when I think of someone who so impacted history. Esther, a supposedly insignificant young lady, changed what could have been a life of misery in the king's house to one of hope. She took her circumstances, which were indeed difficult, and made them into something that could be used for God's purpose. She found favor in the eyes of a king and became his queen. Thus, because of the king's love for her, she was able to save her entire nation. The history she made was explained in Esther 9:27-29: "And that these days should be remembered and kept throughout every generation, every family, every province, and every city; and that these days of Purim should not fail from among the Jews, nor the memorial of them perish from their seed."

What kind of history are you making? Is it a history that your family will look back upon with fondness? Is it a history that they will talk about from now on with their kids and grandkids? Is it a history of which you will be proud? If not, take time today and change the type of history you are making to one of joy and gladness. It goes without saying, but I would much rather be remembered with fond memories than like the one Christmas we shared as a family. Some of the cousins had come to visit us and would not share their toys. It was very frustrating to my girls and to Geoff, my nephew. They eventually left, and as we watched them drive away, Geoff threw his little hands in the air with relief and said with his lisp, "Tank heavens, 'dere gone!"

Make today a happy day. Start your day with a positive and upbeat attitude. Even if you have to work at it, make certain you greet others with a ready smile and kind comment, for whether you realize it or not, you are making history. Make your history count!

We make a living by what we get, we make a life by what we give.
—Winston Churchill

What do we live for if not to make life less difficult for each other?
—George Eliot

*Kara with Dad
and his famous smile*

Are You a Joy Maker?

My children smiling delightedly

With childhood friend, Ronda Hurst, and Kalee at Texas Ladies Conference

Interlude 8

Busy, Busy, Busy

Life is busy, busy, busy. And don't let us forget stressful, stressful, stressful. We are worn out and weary in all of our well-doing.

Recently we had a meeting that involved all the leadership of our constituency. The wives enjoyed getting together for some shopping, eating, and most of all conversation. When women get together, one can bank on it. We will share our thoughts. The conversation revolved around how it seemed we just couldn't get everything done. And because of our efforts to try to cover all the bases, we felt drained and used up. We were "plum tuckered out." Our "iron-poor" blood screams for something to restore us. Thus, we reach for the Geritol.

I read a tidbit about Geritol that should be a blessing to you. It said that Geritol is a combination of the words geriatric and tolerance. So, I looked up the word *geriatric* in the thesaurus on my com-

◈ Are You a Joy Maker?

puter. (How I enjoy clicking on this nifty little mechanism and finding truths galore.) Guess what synonyms popped up? They were "aged, elderly, and old." So one must assume that Geritol was created to help us tolerate getting old. I think I will try to find another source for my vitamins.

Numerous energy drinks have flooded our markets. Red Bull, Powerade, and Fuzion are just a few of the named drinks. One such energy drink that I like is called Propel. I noticed an advertisement in a magazine that showed an individual drinking this fantastic beverage. Just one drop of this amazing tonic made the individual bound off the sidewalk and leap around with unfathomable energy. However, I did not seem to find the same results as what they portrayed. Perhaps I should contact the Better Business Bureau and report the Propel company for false advertisement.

How many times have I heard of someone going to the doctor for an ailment and having the doctor attribute it to stress and overwork. Oh, yes! We live in a busy, busy, busy world.

Times have changed so drastically over the years. I was raised in a small town. I remember as a child coming home from school, practicing my music and getting my homework. Then I would go across the street with my sister to visit our neighbor Fred Geries. He was a wonderful man who had never married because of having to take care of an ailing mother. He would offer us homemade ice cream and fried pies as an after-school snack. Perhaps that is why I have had a weight problem all these years from Fred's chef-like abilities.

Following the snack, we would sit on his porch in those tin-type rocking chairs and watch the people in our neighborhood come home from work. I have such great memories of sitting on his porch during the spring and summer evenings and doing absolutely nothing. How wonderful that sounds! I mean, who has time these days to sit on a porch and do nothing? Sounds like heaven to me.

One would think with all the latest technology and advances that have been made through the years that life would be less stressful and more enjoyable. But I think it has had the reverse effect. All of the technology has instead created a power surge of work.

Several months ago I listened as Pastor Daron Hudspeth spoke of a Congressional Committee that was formed in the 1970s to study what could be done with the amount of leisure time that would be available for Americans in the 2000s. It seemed they believed that at the rate technology was being developed, America would be so highly technologically advanced that there would be much less need for human interaction on the job and around the house. Thus, Americans would need to find something to do to fill all the extra time they would have available.

◎ Are You a Joy Maker?

Just like the statistics not turning out quite as predicted, life does not always turn out as we may think. Thus, the strain of trying to handle all of our responsibilities uses us up.

Logan and Will, grandsons of Marilyn Comeaux, were lying in bed, trying to go to sleep. Their parents were listening to their conversation. Logan, frustrated because he had to go to bed, said, "Oh, God." Will immediately said, "Logan, you can't say that. Nana says you can't say 'God' like that or you will use Him all up."

Of course, we can assume that Nana had told them not to use the Lord's name in vain. Will just had his own interpretation. But there is one thing you can bank on in this life. You will never "use Him all up." He is a constant source of power in our life.

A very familiar Scripture, Matthew 28:18, states it plainly, "And Jesus came and spake unto them, saying, All power is given unto me in heaven and in earth." And in turn, God has given us power through the Holy Ghost. Acts 1:8 says, "But ye shall receive power, after that the Holy Ghost is come upon you: and ye shall be witnesses unto me both in Jerusalem, and in all Judaea, and in Samaria, and unto the uttermost part of the earth." We have been given power by God to change our world and to be witnesses to those around us. We should use this power God has given us.

Busy, Busy, Busy

A young single mother returned home from work one night, along with her four-year-old boy. As she stepped out of the car, two men came up and began attacking her. As she struggled against the men, the little boy slipped inside the house and put on his Power Ranger costume. He came bounding out of the house screaming at the top of his voice, waving his plastic illuminating sword around in the air, and started attacking his mother's assailants. He continued with such force and diligence that he stunned the attackers and kept them at bay until the police arrived. Thankfully, the attackers were caught and brought to justice. When they interviewed the mother and asked her about the situation, she said with a relieved smile, "My son watches the Power Rangers all the time and I guess he thought he had morphed."

Morphed—what a unique word! I entered this word on my thesaurus, thinking I would find a quick synonym, but unfortunately, it did not recognize the word. So, I telephoned my daughter at work since the younger generation keeps up with the latest lingo. To no surprise, Kara did have the definition. Morph means to make a complete change, and even take on a different shape. (Wouldn't it be nice to morph our bodies?) If we could have the faith to believe that we had the power to make a difference in things, just like this little fellow, can you imagine the impact we could have on our world? He showed no fear and was only focusing on his cause to save his mother.

We have a power that lives in us to help us deal with all that life may bring us. He not only promised us power through the Holy Ghost, but He promised us overcoming power. Luke 10:19 states: "Behold, I give unto you power to tread on serpents and scorpions, and over all the power of the enemy: and nothing shall by any means hurt you." The Bible further states in II Timothy 1:7, "For God hath not given us the spirit of fear; but of power, and of love, and of a sound mind."

So when the cares of life weigh us down, let the power of God relieve the stress of your busy, busy, busy life. Become like the little boy and "morph". "And the peace of God, which passeth all understanding, shall keep your hearts and minds through Christ Jesus" (Philippians 4:7).

Shopping with Linda Libby, Corliss Williams, Linda Elms, Diane Stroup, and Pam Pugh

Busy, Busy, Busy

Too busy to speak
Too busy to pray
Too busy to say
"Hey, what's on your mind?"

Too busy to stop
Too busy to stay,
Too busy to find out
"Hey, how's your day?"

Too busy to reach out,
Too busy to share,
Too busy without a doubt
To show someone we care.
—Karla Christian

"Do not pray for easy lives. Pray to be stronger men. Do not pray for tasks equal to your powers. Pray for powers equal to your tasks.
—Phillips Brooks

◐ Are You a Joy Maker?

Kalee and Courtney enjoying Gavin Jones's excitement over our dog, Sugar

Little cousin, Jonathan Haxton, "pondering life"

Interlude 9

I've Got Confidence

We all desire to have a little more confidence. Or at least I do. I envy those people who do not hesitate to express their opinion and actually think everyone is waiting to hear it.

A few years ago my youngest daughter was chosen to be in the St. Louis Children's Choir. We were quite proud of her since she was moved up to a higher level because they thought her voice was so mature for her age. She had to attend practices at the Symphony Powell Hall, a beautiful edifice in St. Louis. It was the type of building that makes you catch your breath in awe when you enter. I was unable to attend, so my husband kindly agreed to take her to the practice. He said he was working while waiting and was faintly aware of the music and practice going in the background. He said he vaguely heard the orchestra and choir leader ask if there were any more questions before dismissing.

⌒ Are You a Joy Maker?

Mark said he then heard a familiar voice and looked down from the balcony. He could not believe what he heard. Here our little eleven-year-old daughter, the youngest one in the choir, was speaking.

"Yes, Kalee," the director said, "did you have a question?"

"Yes, ma'am," said Kalee confidently. "During the last song we sang, I heard some slurring. I thought perhaps we could practice it again."

There was a short silence and then the director said, "You know, Kalee, I think you're right. There was some slurring going on. Let's try that song again."

We have often laughed at the confidence Kalee exhibited that night. She was not the least bit intimidated by the awesome edifice nor the incredible talent that was a part of the upcoming program. All she cared about was the "slurring" she heard, and she wanted it to be right. My husband said he could just imagine the rolling eyes of the other students at the audacity of their youngest choir member.

If we could be that confident in ourselves, it would indeed be great. It would be so nice to walk out the door every morning knowing I looked wonderful. It would be so nice to know that whatever I did would prosper.

Unfortunately, that is not always the case. Not everything goes according to plan. We will encounter unexpected obstacles as we journey through the life we were given. So what is the answer to the dilemma

I've Got Confidence ᴄ⋗

of the confidence factor? One must first have a happy medium of confidence, enough to feel good about oneself without arrogance.

As a girl, I sang in a group called The Soul Searchers. Although the name sounds quite spiritual, we as teenage girls were not always just interested in the spiritual side in searching for souls. We did occasionally search the crowd for good-looking souls who might be in our audience.

Perhaps you have not been impacted by our group yet, so let me give a little more insight into how well known we really were. At one time, we opened for the Oak Ridge Boys when they had a concert in Clovis, New Mexico. Yes, that's right. Of course, that was when their group was still singing gospel music. I know for certain that they still remember the girls' group with big hairdos sporting red, white, and blue polka dot dresses.

One of our favorite numbers was entitled "I've Got Confidence." It was written by the all-time favorite Andre Crouch and was a rather peppy song which seemed to always exude response from the crowd. I was privileged to sing one of the solo stanzas, something about not worrying or fretting. But the key meaning to the whole song was summed up in two lines, "I've got confidence, God is gonna see me through."

Confidence. I looked the word up in the trusty index of my Thompson Chain Reference Study Bible. The majority of the Scriptures referencing "confidence in God" were found in the Book of Psalms. If anyone had confidence in God, it was King David. He had confidence in God when he slew the lion and the bear. He had confidence in God when he slew the giant. He had confidence in God when Saul was pursuing him to destroy him. He had confidence in God when he sinned and knew judgment was coming. He had confidence in God when his children were unruly and Absalom, his son, set out to overthrow him. He had confidence in God, even when his baby was dying.

I could go on and on with the obstacles that continually bombarded the life of David. But he had confidence in his God, the Creator of the universe: "The Lord is my light and my salvation; whom shall I fear? the Lord is the strength of my life; of whom shall I be afraid? . . . Though an host should encamp against me, my heart shall not fear; though war should rise against me, in this will I be confident" (Psalm 27:1, 3).

A few years ago I was diagnosed with a brain aneurysm and chiari malformation. While they were trying to find the diagnosis, I had to lie perfectly still in the MRI machine for almost two and one-half hours. It seemed like an eternity. So, I sang songs in my mind, and this Scripture was one of the songs I sang: "The Lord is my light, and my salvation, whom shall I fear?" (Psalm 27:1). The Lord gave me a song in the night of my life. He gave me something to cling to in the darkness that seemed to surround me.

Psalm 42:8 speaks of the song in the night: "Yet the Lord will command his lovingkindness in the daytime, and in the night his song shall be with me, and my prayer unto the God of my life."

Ironically, the other song I sang while the loud clicking noises surrounded me was "Joy, God's Great Joy." I found it interesting that on several occasions in the Word of God when difficult times were referred to, it also referred to the word *joy* or *gladness*. Isaiah 30:29 says: "Ye shall have a song, as in the night when a holy solemnity is kept; and gladness of heart, as when one goeth with a pipe to come into the mountain of the Lord, to the mighty One of Israel."

During one of our meetings, several of the wives of our general board members of our church organization met at a restaurant to fellowship with a dear lady, Mary Dugas. Mary had recently been diagnosed with an inoperable brain tumor at a stage four. I watched in awe as Mary laughed and talked with us and spoke about the confidence she had in God that everything was going to be all right.

As we walked through a Brighton store looking at various items, she walked toward some of the perfumes that were exhibited. "Karla," she asked, "have you ever tried this perfume? This is my favorite." She picked up the bottle and gave me a sample smell. I immediately agreed with her that it was indeed a wonderful scent. She said, "I not only like the scent, but I like the name as well." As she set the bottle back

∞ Are You a Joy Maker?

down on the counter, I was amazed when one word came into view. It was simply called "Laugh."

This great lady was known for her ability to meet you with a smile and a kind word of encouragement. She was a joy maker. Because of her ability to exude joy, she had already found her song in the night.

So, when those times come when I think no one has as difficult a time as I do, I remember David. And I will remember those, such as Mary Dugas, whom I have been privileged to know, who have passed through my life with confidence and assurance that their "God is gonna see them through."

*My friend,
Mary Dugas*

∞∞∞∞∞∞∞∞∞

I am not afraid of storms, for I am learning how to sail my ship.
—Louisa May Alcott

Interlude 10

Just Needing a Little Attention

Our family sat down at a TGI Friday's to enjoy a meal together before "the Father" once again left town. One of my girls' favorite conversations is to reminisce about things they remembered doing as a child. And to say the least, I am always surprised as they usually share some tidbit I've never heard before. One would think that I should know all there is to know at this point in time since I have three daughters. But alas, they have failed to share everything with "the Mother."

On this cold January evening, Courtney told of one night when we came home late from church, and she felt she needed just a little bit more TLC than normal. So, she feigned sleep while I struggled to disconnect her from the car seat and laboriously hauled her up the stairs. She said I carefully removed her frilly dress and pulled the pajamas over her head. She felt quite proud of herself as the feigned sleep seemed to be working for her. That is, until I removed the frilly socks and she was so ticklish on her feet she could no longer fake sleep. Needless to say, when "the Mother" realized she had been snookered, she was not the least bit happy. All the efforts performed by the "the Mother," hauling the sleeping child up the stairs and the difficulty of removing the clothing, were not small feats. They required a great deal of strength and resilience. So, the child "faking" sleep did not sit well. However, my dear little Courtney felt all the effort was worthwhile, even if "the Mother" gave the child a slight tongue-lashing. The attention and care I showed her was worth it all.

How often in this journey of life do we desire to receive just a little attention from our family or dear friends? When we are experiencing a rather discouraging day, it means so much to us if someone takes the time to show us some attention and remind us they care.

I'm sure the Savior would like for us to give Him some attention on a daily basis. After all He did for us, the least we can do is show Him some attention. Communicating with Him, giving Him praise and adoration, and reading His beloved Word are all ways of showing Him some attention. I hope the Lord doesn't find it necessary to remind me like Courtney did that night with her antics that He needs my attention. I know I can get so focused on the things I feel I need to do that at the end of the day, fatigue and

Just Needing a Little Attention

tiredness make me want to just drag myself to bed. And then I remember I forgot to show the Savior some attention. The cares of life can weigh us down until we may find ourselves going several days before we find the time to commune with Him.

When Kara was about two years of age, she stayed with my mother while I worked. My mother also was so good to help us with things in the home missions church we pastored. One day we were to start a revival, and she was trying to cook a meal for the evangelist that evening before the service. Noticing Kara was looking a bit left out, Mom looked at her and said, "Kara, baby, I am so sorry. Nanaw has been so busy today that she hasn't given you any attention or nothing. Just let me get this dessert finished and I'll read you a book."

Well, Kara picked up on one phrase. From that point on, when she felt left out, she would come up and wrap her little arms around our legs and say "No 'tension, nothing." Yes, it did work. Kara definitely got some attention.

Lord, help me to commune with You and to show You the love You are longing for. I don't want you to have to remind me "I Miss My Time with You." Help me be more attuned to giving You the attention You so deserve. For there are great benefits of being in your presence. Spending time in your presence, Lord, does bring fullness of joy. It is joy unspeakable and full of glory!

Are You a Joy Maker?

The girls enjoying being together

Jonathan, the Joy Maker

Interlude 11

Not Another School Function

Oh, those lovely school assemblies. It seems they come around more often than not. And, if one wants to be a good parent, one must attend. I have attended more than my share with my three girls, believe me. I know the Bible says to give honor where honor is due (Romans 13:7), so I must honor the Word of God and attend the assemblies that give honor to the students (who happen to be my girls).

One fall evening, exhausted from a stressful day of work, I so looked forward to getting home and "chillin' like a villain." But to my amazement, and not a good one at that, Kalee told me the school was sponsoring an assembly and she was so hoping I could go since she had several tests and just could not make it. So, trying to be a good parent and knowing I must show my face in the stead of my daughter, I lumbered out the door with not the best attitude, I'm sorry to say.

☙ Are You a Joy Maker?

I arrived at 6:30, the time I was instructed it started, and found I was one of the first attendees there since it really started at 7:00. Now, I quietly accepted this bump in the road and sat complacently and happy while waiting for others to arrive. (That was not quite my demeanor, but anyway . . .) I was somewhat relieved when the principal finally made the announcement to start the meeting. He graciously introduced the guests as belonging to the Rachel's Challenge endeavor. Of course, I had heard of this young lady, but I had forgotten the details of her life.

Rachel Scott was the first student killed in the Columbine High School killings in 1999. I sat in awe as the representative told of Rachel's goals and her ambitions. One of the statements Rachel often made was that she intended to impact her world. Student after student on the video presentation reiterated her kindness to them and how she always brought so much joy wherever she was. She had written an essay about the necessity of showing compassion and little acts of kindness, and according to the accounts, she did just that. From offering to sit with a new student at lunch to standing up to two buffoons who were bullying a handicapped boy, she seemed to reach out to those around her.

One of the final images that flashed on the screen was her tombstone, which read "She brought so much joy to our lives."

Not Another School Function

A young wisp of a girl became a hero because she believed in making joy not only a part of her life, but tried to bring joy to those around her as well. Thus, the little assembly that I had dreaded was instead an assembly I was so glad to have attended. The tiredness I felt seemed minimal while we viewed images of the darling little girl waving happily at the camera, innocent of what her life would hold. Without any idea whatsoever, she happily left her home that April morning, perhaps thinking she would go about her usual routine at her high school. But her young life was snuffed out so unexpectedly

I remember hearing a song as a child called "What a Difference a Day Makes." The events of a day can change our life for the better, or it can change it for the worse. Although the circumstances were unbelievably violent and horrendous, this family turned a horrible situation into one with a positive solution. They created a program in Rachel's honor that would reach out to the youth of today and share with them how Rachel lived her life to the fullest with the abundance of joy at the forefront. She did indeed impact the world, just as she had always wanted to do.

I have often wondered what people will say about me once I depart from this earthly home. Will they say of me, "We will really miss her. She brought so much joy to everyone."? Or will they breathe a sigh of relief that a cantankerous old soul is finally out of the way?

○○ Are You a Joy Maker?

We should live our lives each day as if it were going to be our last. We should savor the moments we have with our family, with our friends, and always try to look for the good in every situation we encounter. We should live to share that beautiful gift of joy from God.

I enjoy the *Anne of Green Gables* saga. She was one joyful little girl. She lived life with exuberance and resolve. She influenced everyone with her happiness, even an old maid schoolmarm who made her life miserable. Anne was trying to lift the old girl's spirits and give her a shot in the arm. She said, "You need to just keep believing that everything will be fine, that around the next bend in the road is a whole new world for you." The old maid schoolmarm looked back at her as if she had lost her mind and stated emphatically, "There is certainly no bend in my road."[2]

But there is, and you control how you will take that bend in the road. It may not be the bend you expected, but we have the reassurance from the Word of God that He will be with us always. Hebrews 13:5 states, "Let your conversation be without covetousness; and be content with such things as ye have: for he hath said, I will never leave thee, nor forsake thee."

Rachel Scott's young life was cut short, but her family did not let this unexpected tragedy destroy them. Instead they used it as a positive means to teach others, just as their daughter would have wanted. I remember well as the theme flashed across

Not Another School Function

the screen: "Rachel Scott's Joy." What better way to be remembered than by the joyful way she lived life.

So it really wasn't just another school function. It was one school function I was happy to have attended. It was an honor to hear about the life of this young lady. She lived life to the fullest, expecting great things from each day. Rachel Scott was indeed a joy maker.

What you discover when you stop postponing life and start living it, is that happiness comes to those who don't wait!
—Johanna Schilling

---

[2] *http://greengables-2.tripod.com/script*

∾ Are You a Joy Maker?

The Huntley GRANDkids: Christyana, Christian, and Huntley Ballestero

Courtney and Gavin having fun

Interlude 12

I'm Not Perfect

From the time Kalee, our youngest daughter, was old enough to ask, she wanted a puppy. I was able to delay the situation for a time, but then the hubby began to join her cause by reiterating how important it was for a child to have a pet and how much they added to the lives of him and his brothers. So, I finally acquiesced and began searching the papers for a candidate. The only thing Kalee mentioned was that she wanted a dog she could take on walks.

Not very knowledgeable about the attributes of each breed of dog, I coerced the children into considering a pug. After all, if we had to have a dog, it might as well be a cute one. We located a breeder and found the cutest solid black pug with one white stripe down the middle of his flat face. We gave the new addition to the family the name of Sampson. We felt such a name would instill confidence and strength in this black, big-eyed, flat-faced specimen.

◯ Are You a Joy Maker?

Kalee's desire to take him on walks, however, was a disappointment to say the least. We would start out with Sampson on the leash and would only get about a block and a half and the poor dog would start his heavy breathing. Kalee was determined to teach him to go on walks, so we decided to just carry him a while and then let him walk again. To say the least, our walks were indeed a work out for me, as I carried Sampson more than he walked on his own.

Although he was a disappointment in the walking endeavor, Sampson more than made up for it in other areas. He became a much loved dog in our neighborhood. He traveled from house to house to spread his good-natured cheer. We became worried about his not eating, and found out that many in the neighborhood were feeding him steak bones and other goodies. No wonder he wasn't eating his Kibbles and Bits.

Sampson would sit on our front porch daily, waiting for us to get home. When we arrived, he would dash out to the edge of the driveway, make his stance in front of our van, and lead us into the garage, prancing proudly. Although I hate to admit it, I enjoyed watching his antics as much as the girls did.

One day we had to be out of town for a doctor's appointment, and I had made it home barely in time to change clothes for church. We noticed Sampson was not in his usual place, but decided he must be making a neighborhood visit. We had just gotten in the house when our doorbell rang. It was one of our

I'm Not Perfect

neighbor friends who had a sad expression on her face. She looked at the girls and me and said, "I so hate to be the bearer of bad news, but Sampson was run over today by the Mail Lady. I have him over at my house, and he is in pretty bad shape."

Well, the girls, especially Kalee, were devastated. We went to her house and as we walked the block and a half, we were joined by other neighbors who already knew about Sampson. When we arrived at her house, it was amazing to me that the whole neighborhood had come to see him as well. He lay prostrate on her deck and could not move anything except his little round head. When he saw Kalee, his big huge eyes lit up and he tried to get up, but just could not rise. Of course, Kalee started bawling when she saw his condition. The neighbors knew that my husband was a pastor, so I explained that since he was out of town, I would need to attend church. The kind lady told me to go ahead and go to church and I could stop by afterward to pick him up.

I didn't want to take him to an emergency vet as it looked like he wouldn't survive anyway, so Mark and I decided to just wait until the morning and then take him in. Miraculously, the sturdy Sampson survived the night. I suppose he lived up to his name after all. I took him to the vet and they placed an ID band around his neck and told me they would keep him to find out what all was wrong. I called all day long to check on him, and the vet said that he was

Are You a Joy Maker?

doing amazingly well. They thought he might have internal bleeding, but he had no broken bones.

To make a long story short, Sampson returned home in a battered condition and limped around for several weeks. But it wasn't long before he was again back to normal. The neighbors were so excited that he had survived that he received better treatment than ever before. He became quite spoiled. One little, fat black dog helped those in our neighborhood become better acquainted and better friends. We were only passing acquaintances of the lady who found him and kept him for us. But after the accident, we found out what awesome neighbors they really were.

How often have we hoped or desired to be something other than what we are? It is our human nature to see our imperfections more so than our good points. Although we should never be egotistical or arrogant, God expects us to take what He has given us and use it for His glory, as well as to accept what He has given us. I am far from perfect, but I try in the best way possible to use what I have to further His kingdom.

Pastor J. T. Pugh once said, "Every man I meet is in some way my better." In other words, there is always going to be someone who can out do you. On the other hand, you have things available in your life that you can do better than someone else. If we combine our efforts for the kingdom, we could accomplish great things.

I'm Not Perfect

It's just like our little fat pug, who never could become a walking dog, but became so much more. He became a favorite in our neighborhood with his antics and his friendliness. We only found that out because he had been hurt. It is not easy to hurt, but his being hurt caused us to meet neighbors we had never known before. Old Sampson was the instigator of our benefits. No, he was not perfect, but he made up for his imperfections in so many other ways that his not doing so well as our walking dog dimmed in comparison to all the other fun he gave us.

So, if you're thinking that you will never be what you want to be, perhaps God has something else in mind for you. He has another path he wants you to embark upon, and you will find greater things beyond your wildest imagination. Put your life into the Master's hand.

The "not-so-perfect" dog

Are You a Joy Maker?

"God is my strength and power: and he maketh my way perfect" (II Samuel 22:33).

"But the God of all grace, who hath called us unto his eternal glory by Christ Jesus, after that ye have suffered a while, make you perfect, stablish, strengthen, settle you" (I Peter 5:10).

The farther a man knows himself to be free from perfection, the nearer he is to it.
—Gerard Groote

Interlude 13

A Friend Indeed

My cell phone rang and I looked down, smiling when I saw my sister's familiar number. Our normal conversation commenced:
"Hey, how are you?"
"Great, how are you?"
"Good, so what are you doing?"
"Oh, nothing, what are you doing?"
"Oh, nothing."

Now I know this conversation is very intriguing, but I must stop the train of thought I'm following here.

Vicki had indeed called to tell me a funny story. She and her husband Joe almost daily make a scheduled stop at their local Sonic Drive-In to purchase a large Diet Coke and a large Diet Cherry Limeade. They were often served by a young man who became quite familiar with their order. Joe often teased the

Are You a Joy Maker?

young man, and they enjoyed exchanging barbs. A friendship ensued.

On a scheduled visit, they gave their normal order and awaited their delectable beverages. They were discussing the day's events when they heard someone knocking on a window. Looking up they spotted their faithful carrier in the window holding up a sign that said "Howdy" and waving in greeting. Since someone else was up to deliver their drinks, he wanted to at least say "Hello" to his friends and found an unusual way of doing so. Vicki said that the manager came up behind him to see what he was doing, and instead of reprimanding him, began laughing when he saw the sign the young man had prepared. So, although their acquaintance was simply through the Sonic, the young man enjoyed seeing them every day and looked forward to their visits.

Other such occurrences came to my mind following my conversation with Vicki. A few days following our International General Conference, we decided to take a few days off with our good friends, Jerry and Phyllis Jones. Once on the road, we decided to stop for a bite of breakfast in the town in which we used to pastor, Winston-Salem, North Carolina. We guided them to the IHOP restaurant we had frequented while living there. Much to my surprise, the lady who had been manager when we left seven years before was still there. Her face lit up and she

A Friend Indeed

gave me a quick hug, expressing how nice it was to see us once again. She asked how the girls were and shared some updates of her own as well.

Our friends could not believe it. They never failed to tease us about our restaurant ministry and always knowing the management, so when the lady remembered us from living in Winston several years before, the Joneses could not let it go by without giving us a hard time.

I am amazed often at the kindness and concern shown by people who don't even know us very well, simply because we took the time to speak and show an interest in their lives. And do you know it doesn't cost anything but time to make a friend? In this day and time, everyone is looking for something that does not cost anything. And I know of nothing more rewarding than having good friends and making new friends as well.

Our middle daughter, Courtney, was required to make several weekend trips with the chorale at her university in order to fulfill a scholarship she was awarded. The students at the university were well aware of Courtney's religious beliefs and were kind and gracious enough to accept them as her commitment to God. They stopped in one small town several hours away from St. Louis to get a bite to eat following their concert. Being a small town, the Pizza Hut seemed the best choice to curb their hunger pangs. They walked in, and while waiting to

Are You a Joy Maker?

order, some of the kids were biding their time by reading the bulletin board.

Suddenly, one of the guys said, "Hey, Courtney, here are some people like you." Courtney walked over to the bulletin board and saw a picture of the local pastor and his family.

"Oh, yes," she said, "That's Pastor Calvin Jean and his family." A hush fell over the group.

Then one of the girls exclaimed, "You know these people?"

"Certainly," Courtney responded. "They pastor here in this town." Everyone started laughing and Courtney looked at them with a puzzled expression.

"What's wrong?" she asked innocently.

One guy answered, "You mean to tell me that we are two hours away from home in this small, insignificant town and you know people here, too? Do you know someone in every town that we go to?"

Remembering that this had happened on other occasions, Courtney smiled and answered, "I probably do if they are Pentecostal. Pentecostals have friends everywhere."

How true that statement is! We really do have friends everywhere. And as the students so aptly portrayed, it is easy to spot our friends. It is not very difficult to know that we belong to the kingdom of God. However, although we enjoy such wonderful friendships within our constituency, we should never overlook the chance to make friends with others as well, whether it is the server at a restaurant, the bank teller, or the clerk at the grocery store. Jesus cares about them all.

While Kara, our oldest daughter, was attending college, she had the chance to make a lot of friends. One such friend she became acquainted with was Patricia. Patricia had experienced some difficulties in her life and was trying her best to make a success of things in spite of the unfairness that had come her way. Kara continued to pursue the friendship, and often times I would hear her on the phone with Patricia inviting her to church and trying to help her with situations in her life. Eventually, Patricia visited church with us, and Kara began a Bible study with her.

Due to the necessity of travels for our family, we put Patricia in contact with our very dear friends, the Tom Trimble family. They surrounded Patricia with love and continued with Bible studies and Christian character classes. What a joy it was that Sunday when we received the call from a very happy Patricia announcing that she had received the Holy Ghost! She was baptized as well and has become an absolutely outstanding woman of God. Patricia came with me to church last Sunday, and I watched in thankfulness as she worshipped and shouted and praised God with all her being. You see, before Patricia found God, she had surrounded herself with barriers to counteract the hurt that had bombarded her life. But now that she has found the Friend

⌒ Are You a Joy Maker?

above all friends, she can worship with abandonment and hope. Patricia amazes me at the maturity of her faith and the hope she has for her future. Kara made a friend and led her friend to the greatest Hope she could ever find.

Jesus was always interested in making friends. He ate with publicans and sinners. He befriended a tax cheat. He talked with a woman of ill repute alone at a well. He even stood up for a woman accused of adultery in front of those who considered themselves holy. Yes, He did make new friends at the cost of ruining His own reputation. But all that mattered to the Savior was reaching a hungry soul.

As I was reading the verses relating to these instances, I found that the Savior's endeavors were indeed successful. : "And it came to pass, that, as Jesus sat at meat in his house, many publicans and sinners sat also together with Jesus and his disciples: for there were many, and they followed him." There is nothing more inspiring than those few words: "and they followed him."

My desire as I traverse through this world is to make friends, and while making friends, influence those friends to follow Him. The best gift you could ever give a friend is to introduce him or her to the Greatest Friend he or she will ever have. Jesus will become his or her Friend indeed.

A Friend Indeed

*Patricia and
Kara, true friends*

"A man that hath **friends** must shew himself **friendly**: and there is a **friend** that sticketh closer than a brother" (Proverbs 18:24).

A real friend is one who walks in when the rest of the world walks out.
—Walter Winchell

◯ Are You a Joy Maker?

Another set of true friends, Phyllis and I

Gavin Jones
in bubbles of joy

Interlude 14

What's It Worth to You?

I am a bit peeved this cold December evening. Okay, I'll just be honest here, since it is the best policy. I am quite put out! I have just completed assisting my daughter with a gargantuan school project, and in spite of the late, or rather early, hour, I am too keyed up to sleep. So I decided to muse about the project dilemma.

Now I understand that the intention of a project is to provide quality time for the child and parent to bond. I don't think so! Not much bonding going on here. I spend my supposedly quality time frustrated at the momentous amount of work involved and am only focusing on getting finished. I don't think teachers realize that the explanation of a project that takes maybe three to five minutes actually entails a minimum of 72 hours of continuous stress, paperwork, and graphics, not counting the hours of research as well.

ᴐ͂ Are You a Joy Maker?

And even more special is if the teacher partners your child with someone who has no inclination to do their part of the project. Yes, this is promoting interaction all right. It teaches your child that it is their job to get everything together, do all the work, and turn in a nicely completed project with both students' names attached. So the inactive student gets a tremendous grade without doing one thing! Wow! That is really teaching the sloth how to get along in life! But don't you dare say a word to cast a reflection on the silent and inactive student as that would be tattling and the teacher doesn't like tattling. Sounds like the teacher is adhering more to teaching biblical principles of suffering in silence, or turning the other cheek. It makes me end up praying for those who despitefully use me, or rather the daughter, of course. So many Scriptures come to mind at this point, but I just don't have time to share them all.

So why do I continue to help with these seemingly impossible projects? Because my daughter wants to make an A. Making A's means a great deal to her as she wants to go to an Ivy League university, and having A's helps get scholarships, and scholarships give the parent money. So, yes, I will still help with all projects. Not happy about it, but it is worth the effort, according to the daughter.

Oh, yes, I am well aware I do have an attitude and should probably go immediately to sign up for that next seminar entitled, "The Strong-Willed and Mad Parent." Although I fuss and stew and spew forth threatenings, I will continue to assist the child with whatever I can as I also want her to succeed and reach that goal she has set for her life. So, yes, it is worth it.

Even more important than helping our children succeed educationally is the responsibility of teaching them how to live for God. Everything else in life pales in comparison to the ultimate reason for our being here. The Word of God tells us "For God so loved the world, that he gave his only begotten Son, that whosoever believeth in him should not perish, but have everlasting life" (John 3:16). God loved us so much that He gave everything He had—His own life. And, it is our responsibility to teach them that if they live for Him and believe in Him, that they will not perish, but have a life in Him far beyond what they can imagine.

Perhaps the best way to teach our kids to live for God is by example. I grew up in a small town and spent nearly more time at church than I did at home. It seemed if we weren't at church making peanut brittle or at the local civic hall having a Mexican dinner, we were cleaning the church or helping my mother prepare for children's church on Sunday. It seemed it was always church, church, church. But I did not mind because my parents made it fun. We went to every fellowship meeting, every youth rally,

◌ Are You a Joy Maker?

every youth camp, and every camp meeting. We spent many vacations on the old campground.

But unfortunately, times have changed. I have often heard the comment (of which I am unfortunately guilty): "I don't intend to spend the only time I have off in a church camp meeting." Now, I would be the first to say that church does consume a great deal of our time, but what cause is more important than the cause of Christ? I received a cute email that said, "I Too Am a Drug Addict." I opened the email and began to smile as I identified with the words.

"The other day, a friend in my town read that a Meth lab had been found in an old farmhouse in the adjoining county. He turned to me and asked me a rhetorical question: 'Why didn't we have a drug problem when you and I were growing up?' I told him that I did have a drug problem when I was young: I was drug to church on Sunday morning. I was drug to church for weddings and funerals. I was drug to family reunions and community socials no matter the weather. I was drug by my ears when I was disrespectful to adults. I was also drug to the woodshed when I disobeyed my parents, told a lie, brought home a bad report card, did not speak with respect, spoke ill of the teacher or the preacher, or if I didn't put forth my best effort in everything that was asked of me. I was drug to the kitchen sink to have my mouth washed out with soap if I uttered a profanity. I was drug out to pull weeds in mom's gar-

What's It Worth to You?

den and flowerbeds and cockleburs out of dad's fields. I was drug to the homes of family, friends, and neighbors to help some poor soul who had no one to mow the yard, repair the clothesline, or chop some firewood; and, if my mother had ever known that I took a single dime as a tip for this kindness, she would have drug me back to the woodshed.

"Those drugs are still in my veins and they affect my behavior in everything I do, say, or think. They are stronger than cocaine, crack, or heroin; and, if today's kids had this kind of drug problem, America would be a better place."

Yes, I am also a drug addict due to the example of my parents. And I, along with my husband, seem to be carrying on the tradition. My husband and I are making drug addicts out of our girls as well. We drug them to church early for choir practice or praise singer practice as little tykes. We drug them to church when they were sick with sore throats or something that hopefully was not contagious. I drug them to all the children's musical practices and made them play parts they did not want to play. My husband drug them to visit people with him. We drug them to all of our district events. And we are still dragging them around, asking them to help with promotions, packing, and whatever else we feel is necessary for us to work in our field of labor. I honestly don't think they could function normally if they did not have church. I know I couldn't.

◈ Are You a Joy Maker?

There seems to be a spirit threatening the lives of our kids. Our older children face a world of drugs, drinking, and bad language on a daily basis as they walk the halls of their schools. Now our younger children face the threat of abductors and kidnappers. They cannot trust even the friendly smile of a passerby because that stranger may be a bad person.

We need to bombard the gates of Hell with much prayer and supplication on behalf of our children. The enemy is surrounding them with enticements and luring them with images of a better life other than through God. We need to pray that God will surround them with His protection and love. We need to pray that they will be able to sustain the onslaught of the enemy when he comes against them as a roaring lion, seeking to devour.

However, we do not want to make fear the object of their minds. In our teaching, we should warn them of the obstacles they face, but emphasize that they should not fear. They have a God who watches over them night and day. He will go to battle for them against the enemy of this world. Teach them that Jesus can do all things. He can protect. He can help them whenever they are afraid, and He can bring peace to their minds and hearts.

I heard an interesting commentary about a child's parents who were not getting any sleep at night because their little boy was afraid of monsters and goblins in the closet. They came up with the

What's It Worth to You?

idea of developing a colorful spray bottle of fragrant mist, and whenever the child came to them, they would use the spray bottle to get rid of the monsters and goblins. It worked so well with their son that they are now marketing their product. The reporter said that it was amazing how well it is selling.

A friend of mine, Joy Norris, was on her way to church one Sunday morning, and as is usual for most of us, she was running late and in a hurry. In her anticipation of getting there on time, she almost had a wreck. She immediately called out "Jesus" as the car skidded. Thankfully, she avoided the mishap and continued on to church, somewhat unnerved. However, in Sunday school class, when the teacher asked if anyone had a prayer request, little Tyler Cole raised his hand and said, "We need to pray for Jesus this morning. I think my Mommy ran over Him."

We need to teach and be an example that when difficulties come, call on the name above all names, *Jesus*! We don't have to use a spray bottle of fragrant mist that consists of nothing to alleviate our fears. Let your children know they can call on Jesus.

A kindergarten teacher was observing her classroom of children while they were drawing. She would occasionally walk around to see each child's work. As she got to one little girl who was diligently working, she asked what her drawing was. The girl replied, "I'm drawing God." The teacher paused and

༄ Are You a Joy Maker?

said, "But no one knows what God looks like." Without missing a beat, or looking up from her drawing, the girl replied, "They will in a minute."

Teaching your child to live for God is the most important lesson you will ever teach them. Teach them to develop such a close relationship with Him that just like this little girl, they feel they know what He looks like, even though they have never seen Him. Teaching them to be able to trust and believe God for anything is a gift beyond words.

Some years ago when the girls were still small, my husband was preaching a rather difficult meeting. There were some problems in the district where he was, and it was affecting the night services. He kept mentioning to me on the phone his need of the Lord's guidance. I knew about what time he was going to preach, so I called Kara, Courtney, and Kalee to my room and said, "Girls, Dad really needs our prayers right now. He is going to be preaching in just a few minutes and needs the Lord's help." Within just a few minutes, the tears were flowing and the older two were speaking in that heavenly language. After we finished praying, Kalee (a new convert at the age of five), said confidently, "He is going to be okay." And she was right. My husband told me later that just a few hours after we prayed, a mighty move of the Spirit entered that place and God intervened in that difficult situation. All because our kids prayed and believed God would intervene.

What's It Worth to You?

What a challenge as parents we have assumed in having children! However, we have the privilege of molding and influencing the church of tomorrow through our children. Oh, yes, it is important to prepare them for the world with education and knowledge, but it is so much more important that we teach them how to serve God.

Bill Gates made a statement in *Time Magazine* several years ago that struck my heart. He said, "Just in terms of allocation of time resources, religion is not very efficient. There's a lot more I could be doing on Sunday morning." Obviously, he did not have a very pleasant church experience and that is sad indeed.

We need to teach our kids that church is a pleasant experience. We need to teach our kids that Jesus is the only way. We need to teach them that the very best friend they will ever have is Jesus Christ. We need to teach our kids to look for the good in things instead of the negative. We need to teach our kids to have a positive attitude and greet each day with the joy of the Lord. If we take the time to teach them how to serve God, it will be worth everything. For if we serve Him together here, we can live with Him together forever over there! *It will be worth it all . . . so let us run this race, 'til we see Christ.*

༄ Are You a Joy Maker?

My sister, Vicki, with grandson, Alex

Vicki, Kara, and I enjoy a joyful moment

Interlude 15

That's All That Matters

It was a dark and stormy night. A small, menacing figure exited the brightly lit structure and peered anxiously into the night. Glancing quickly to the right and left, the moonlight caught her exquisite features as she ran into the shrouded fog. Her quick footsteps echoed across the pavement as she continued glancing furtively all around. For what seemed like an eternity, she continued past vehicle after vehicle until she spotted the looming, black SUV located at the farthest end of the parking lot. Clicking the automatic opener, she sighed in relief as the red lights blinked invitingly through the haze. Picking up the pace, she glanced around once again, opened the door, and quickly jumped into the secure haven while breathing a sigh of relief.

Shaking with fear, she finally found the ignition and started the vehicle. Driving toward the entrance of the same building she had exited, she pulled into

↭ Are You a Joy Maker?

the lit driveway. At that precise moment, a beautiful, blonde young lady hurried out the door, grasping the arm of a well-dressed gentleman. The shrouded light caught his features, evidencing the pain he was experiencing. The young lady gently assisted him into the passenger seat and rapidly moved to enter the back of the vehicle. Then with hardly a second to spare, the black luminous car sped away into the night.

Oh, how I wish the above scenario was as intriguing as it sounds. However, I must veer away from the creative fiction side of my writing and tell it like it really happened. It was indeed a rainy night, and the menacing figure exiting the brightly lit building was, sad to say, me. Now, I certainly don't consider my features exquisite, but it at least got your attention. My footsteps were quick, that's for certain, as I tried to find where my husband had parked his "rig." Since he was the last driver, I knew almost certainly that he would have parked our SUV at the farthest point on the parking lot so as not to have uncaring drivers bang their doors against our car. I wish just this one time he had parked a bit closer. I was relieved when I saw the blinking red lights indicating the location of our car, and I was so glad when I finally got inside.

I was shaking, that's for sure, because I was very apprehensive about a situation that had just occurred. Bear with me as I continue this repertoire. I drove to the door and the beautiful, blonde young lady, which was my daughter, helped the well-dressed gentleman, which was my husband, into the front seat. And it was quite evident that he was in pain, which was displayed quite profoundly in his handsome features. Thus our trek began that fateful night.

Let me review a bit. We were out of town at a ladies conference in Charlotte, North Carolina, when much to our surprise my husband became overwhelmed with unbearable pain. Not one to ever be ill, I became quite concerned and called 911. The paramedics arrived quickly and did a preliminary heart test, which thankfully showed nothing to be wrong. Thus, my dear, wonderful husband refused to ride in the ambulance to the hospital. Instead, he appointed me to be his designated driver. Thus, my hike across the parking lot to retrieve the transportation.

One small fact I failed to mention was that a trailer was attached to our vehicle, which I had never driven up to this point. And to make matters worse, the rain was coming down at a steady pace. Now you know why I was shaking!

We entered the hospital address into the GPS of our trusty Navigator, and it gave explicit directions to the hospital. (Thank the Lord!) However, the pain worsened as I drove. So, here I am, very inexperienced, driving at a breakneck speed through the pouring rain to a place I had never been before. With, may I add, my husband praying and asking "How much further?" every few seconds. I have

☙ Are You a Joy Maker?

never been happier to see a familiar hospital sign pointing me in the right direction. I roared into the emergency entrance, and the beautiful, blonde young lady helped my pain-driven husband out of the car while I went to park. Needless to say, I did not park at the farthest point of the lot.

The medical personnel had trouble finding some pain medication that would relieve the hubby's pain. And I was very concerned because my dear, sweet man had a high tolerance for pain, so something was definitely wrong. After running test after test, they could not pinpoint any certain diagnosis. The doctor was very concerned because the pain was so intense, and she was certain something was wrong, even quoting dire possibilities to us. After several days of testing, we waited and waited for some results, not knowing what to expect. Discussion after discussion ensued before the final diagnosis. My husband had multiple gallstones. Now to say we were relieved might be somewhat odd. But we were very relieved since it was the best possible diagnosis for which we could hope. One might say we were glad for gallstones.

All joking aside, one never knows what a day will bring. Within moments our lives could change due to an unexpected death, a diagnosis of a severe illness, or losing a job into which we have poured our lives. However, God does not want us to live in a constant state of anxiety waiting for the worst to happen.

That's All That Matters

In Deuteronomy 31, Moses knew his time on this earth was almost over. I'm certain the man felt a bit saddened that he was not going to be able to lead God's people into the land of promise. When the children of Israel started their journey from the land of Egypt, Moses had no idea it was going to take such a long time to reach what was promised them. Unfortunately, their human natures kept them from reaching their goal sooner. It is so difficult sometimes to get this flesh of ours under subjection to the will of God. Thus, God has to take us to places we really don't want to go in order to bring us to what He wants us to be. So, the children of Israel wandered from place to place, dealing with adversity after adversity, when if only they had submitted to God's will, they could have reached their goal much sooner.

I probably would not have made a very good Israelite as I want things to happen now and be completed as quickly as possible. I am so adamant about things that my girls in fact have nicknamed me "Turbo Mom." No, patience is not one of my virtues. I cannot imagine having to wander around for forty years trying to get to some place I could have been a long time before.

Thus, Moses had to pass leadership to Joshua to lead the people on to the promise. He spoke to the people a word of encouragement I have referred to many times, "Be strong and of a good courage, fear not, nor be afraid of them: for the Lord thy God, he

◯ Are You a Joy Maker?

it is that doth go with thee; he will not fail thee, nor forsake thee" (Deuteronomy 31:6).

What a promise and hope we have in Him. No matter what the day may bring your way, you can have hope in the Lord. He will not fail us, and He will not forsake us. He told us to "be strong and of a good courage" and to "fear not."

The story is told that during a rescue of a Nazi concentration camp, Allied soldiers came into a dank prison cell and found a statement scrawled on the wall: "I believe in the sun even when it is not shining . . . in love even when I am alone . . . and in God even when He is silent."[3]

The struggles we face are not easy. There may be times we don't understand why God seems so far away. During those times we must hold fast to His nail-scarred hand. For whether we feel His presence or not, He is there. When nothing seems to be going right or nothing seems blessed, remember that our tenure here is only temporary: the house, our cars, our business success. The things of this world are not what it is all about.

I once read a statement that said, "We only have but maybe a blink here on earth." Such a short, short time. Whatever I do in that blink of time, I want to matter for eternity. I want to affect things in a positive manner, whatever time God has allowed me. I want to enjoy serving the Lord, and when things come my way I didn't plan on, I will still believe in

That's All That Matters

God. When gallstones appear, I will still believe in God. He is my anchor and He is my hope. He will get me through any situation.

Pastor J. T. Pugh read a poem quite frequently that gave me such inspiration.

Crossing the Bar

Sunset and evening star,
And one clear call for me!
And may there be no moaning of the bar,
When I put out to sea,

But such a tide as moving seems asleep,
Too full for sound and foam,
When that which drew from out the boundless deep
Turns again home.

Twilight and evening bell,
And after that the dark!
And may there be no sadness of farewell,
When I embark;

For tho' from out our bourne of Time and Place
The flood may bear me far,
I hope to see my Pilot face to face
When I have crossed the bar.

—Alfred Lord Tennyson

◠ Are You a Joy Maker?

And when life is over, I look forward to Him greeting me with open arms. Revelations 1:17 says, "And when I saw him, I fell at his feet as dead. And he laid his right hand upon me, saying unto me, Fear not; I am the first and the last." He is our first and last, and that is all that matters.

Each day is a promise
of new joys to gain
if we look for the rainbow
instead of the rain.
There's never a winter that will not end,
never a tree too strong to bend,
never a sky too dull and gray
To change—given time—to a brighter day!

—Unknown

---

[3] *http://www.baldwincountynow.com*

Interlude 16

Reach out and Touch

I am often accused of having a song for every situation, especially by my friend, Diana Jolley. She will make some random statement, and I will break forth into song. She has gotten quite used to my antics and has learned to brace herself for the coming rendition. It just seems that the smallest phrase will set me off into song. Now, they are not always gospel tunes, but songs that I have heard through the years. One such song I do remember was a song entitled "Reach out and Touch." Even AT&T made use of that song title in hopes of encouraging people to buy their phone service. I can still remember the words quite well!

Reach out and touch somebody's hand
Make this world a better place if you can.

⏾ Are You a Joy Maker?

In this world of uncertainty and fear, all we have to hold on to is our God and those around us. I don't want to live my days only looking out for me, but I want to "reach out and touch" those around me. I don't want to live as if I am the center of the universe. And we have met more than our share of those types of people. When we meet someone who treats us arrogantly, my husband often quotes, "Bow down and worship me." I do not want to present the image that I expect special treatment or need special attention.

I once read an article about C. W. Metcalf, a great storyteller in his own right. He said that he was in an airport and saw a man who was verbally abusing an airline ticketing agent. The traveler had missed his flight due to mechanical difficulties and was being loud, aggressive, and just plain mean to the poor ticketing agent, who obviously had no control over the plane's condition. Metcalf went up to the abusive man and asked, "Can I have your autograph?" When the man, puzzled, asked, "Why do you want my autograph?" Metcalf responded, "Because I've never met the center of the universe before!"

Oh, how I would love to do something like that sometimes! It makes me want to respond like I see the youth of today do so often: raised fist in the air, pulled down with strength, and uttering "Yes!" Life is going to hand us detours and bumps along the way, and even closed roads and cancelled flights. How we handle those unexpected occurrences will show what kind of Christians we really are.

I was on my way to speak at a ladies conference in Little Rock, Arkansas, and had gone through the hassle of checking my bags, going through the long line at security, and finally arriving at my designated gate. The plane was running late, and the announcement was made, "This is a full flight, as well as a connecting flight. So if you would, please, hurry onto the plane and take the closest seat you can find so that we can be on our way."

"Okay, sure," I thought, joining the rest of the disgruntled passengers on the plane. Of course, there were no seats available but middle seats, and I was so excited! I mean, everyone likes middle seats, don't they? So, with a smile on my face, I started down the aisle. Catching the eye of one gentleman right at the front of the plane, he asked, "Would you like to sit here?" Surprised that he would actually invite me to sit down, I graciously said, "Sure." He helped me put down my things, and I scrunched past him to my middle seat. I had no more than sat down when he asked, "Got any peanut brittle?"

Surprised, I looked at him. Before I could answer, the man to my left leaned forward and said, "Now that wasn't a nice way to greet this lady. What are you thinking?"

"Well," the man answered, "I figured she was Pentecostal and she might have a little peanut brittle for us."

◌ Are You a Joy Maker?

Of course, I laughed. The man quickly said to his friend, "Now see there! That's why we chose her to sit here." Then he looked at me and said, "My friend here and I decided we were going to choose our next flying partner since the last guy who sat here was a real grump."

The two men introduced themselves and said that they worked for Anheuser Busch. I introduced myself to them as well, and then the more chatty guy said, "Really, I didn't mean to offend you with my peanut brittle comment. I just know we like the Pentecostals' peanut brittle. By the way, we're Catholic."

"Oh, I wasn't offended," I answered. "I thought it was funny. But, you have to admit the Catholics have their own fundraisers as well. You know, like bingo."

Both men laughed, and one added, "Yes, and spaghetti suppers."

We talked and laughed most of the way through the turbulent flight to Little Rock. Then just as we were landing, the pilot suddenly accelerated the plane and we started a sharp climb back into the sky. I felt like I was on the space shuttle. Now, being one who doesn't like to fly that well anyway, I automatically uttered, "Jesus!" The men glanced at me, but didn't say anything. Continuing to pray quietly, I was so relieved when the pilot came on the intercom. "Sorry about that, folks. We were just fixing to land when ground control notified us that there was a tornado on the ground headed toward the terminal. We had to put her back in the air as soon as possible. So, unfortunately, we are going to have to re-route to Dallas because of the weather." All around you could hear the people's responses of "Oh, no!"

What should have been a fifty-minute flight ended up being a five-hour flight. Now, you can imagine the discontent among the passengers, but not in our area. There were two rows of us who shared stories, jokes, and just had a good time. We talked about our families, and the kind gentleman on my left expressed an interest in my beliefs. I had a chance to share this greatest experience with him and told him of the peace I had found through Jesus.

When we finally landed back in Little Rock, the one gentleman on my right said, "Thanks for sitting with us and making this long flight more enjoyable. You taught us how to pray and have fun at the same time." Then he pointed his finger at me and said, "Let me tell you something, little lady, I have changed my mind about you Pentecostals."

When we have those unexpected incidences, don't become irate and grumpy, trying to show you are the center of the universe. Look around and reach out to those around you. Try to bring some joy into their otherwise stressed existence.

I have a wonderful friend, Phyllis Jones, who goes far and beyond what she should to reach out to others. I was with her at a McDonald's drive-through one day, and we were talking about the stress people

Are You a Joy Maker?

were going through. "Just look at that lady behind us. She probably has several kids and looks like she could use a break."

When she pulled up to the drive-through window to pay, she told the attendant, "I would like to also pay for the car's order behind me."

The attendant looked puzzled, and she asked, "Do you have the total of their order?"

"Uh, yes," the attendant said.

"Well, then," Phyllis answered, "just add that amount to my order."

The attendant did as she said, and as we drove away, Phyllis said, "I hope I helped her day improve."

Just a simple act of kindness, but it probably brought a smile to the lips of that little lady behind us. Don't try to make yourself the center of the universe, but show them the true Center of the universe. Show them that Jesus can be the center of their joy. Make an effort to reach out and touch the lives of those around you. You may be the only way they ever see Jesus. So, I will conclude with the ending of that song:

Reach out and touch somebody's hand
Make this world a better place if you can.
Just try . . .

Interlude 17

Who Do You Think You Are?

Waiting to board a plane, I noticed a group of people gathered around four rather attractive young women. They were snapping pictures with them, obtaining their autographs, and gushing over them. I didn't seem to recognize any of them and since I know just about everyone, I was quite frustrated by my ignorance. An airline pilot behind me asked if I knew who they were (since I'm sure I exuded the air that I did know everyone). I assured him that I had no idea. Finally, after the crowd had cleared and the girls had gone, he went up to someone in the group that had been gathered around them and asked who the girls were. "Oh," the girl answered, "they were Dallas Cowboys cheerleaders."

The world is in awe of celebrities and superstars. Anyone who is the slightest bit famous is of interest to us. And we try our best to be just as impressive as they are.

∽ Are You a Joy Maker?

I was privileged to have Pastor and Mrs. Royce Elms in Amarillo, Texas, as my pastor for a period of time during my teen years. Sister Elms is quite a lady and has had several interesting things happen to her. I heard Pastor Elms tell of one occasion when he decided to take his wife to an upscale restaurant in Amarillo, Texas. He said as they were being led to their table, he noticed a number of servers hovering around a nearby table, and much to his surprise realized it was a well-known country singer. He brought the matter to Sister Elms' attention, and they talked about it a few moments and then turned their attention to their menu choices. They ordered their meals and were told they could go to the salad bar. They got up and started toward the bar. Brother Elms said that he usually allowed Sister Elms to go first, but for some reason he was leading the way this night. He said they had to pass the table of the well-known artist. In their pursuit of their goodies, they heard some glasses falling, plates falling, and other paraphernalia turning over. He said he couldn't figure out where all the noise was coming from and stopped to look back at Sister Elms. To his dismay, he saw that Sister Elms had inadvertently tucked their tablecloth into the band of her skirt, pulled everything off their table setting, and had dragged the table cloth right by this famous person's table. He said he glanced in the man's direction and he was politely trying to hide his laughter. It was a humbling experience indeed for them.

Unfortunately, our human nature is one that does like some type of recognition. When someone recognizes us, it just gives us a little bit of "umph." It gives us a boost in our egos that makes us feel like "Hey, I really do matter here."

At a general conference a few years back, my friends Phyllis Jones, Pam Pugh, and I got on an elevator with some very nice people. We spoke and they returned our greetings. Then one man asked, "So where are you ladies from?" Phyllis answered, "I'm Phyllis Jones, and I'm from St. Louis, Missouri."

"Jones?" the man asked. "From St. Louis?"

"Yes," she responded.

"Are you kin to Reverend Jerry Jones?" he asked.

"Well, yes," she admitted, looking rather shy. "That's my husband."

"Oh, my!" he responded. Then he turned to his family and friends. "Do you know who this is?" he asked with excitement. "This is the wife of Brother Jerry Jones, our general secretary. This is Sister Jones."

Then being the good friend she is, she started trying to shift the focus off of herself and onto Pam and me. "This is Karla Christian, and her husband is the marketing director. And this is Pam Pugh; her husband is superintendent of Texico District, and she is the daughter-in-law of J. T. Pugh." Oh, there

∞ Are You a Joy Maker?

was so much handshaking going on as the wonderful people acted overwhelmed to meet us. It was humbling to say the least. And, it did make us feel important, even if for a brief moment.

Amid all the accolades and acknowledgment, a small voice cried out in the din of noise. "Hey, we aren't moving." One of their small children brought us back to reality. In the middle of all their kindness, we had forgotten to push the elevator button indicating what floor we wanted. We were still on the first floor.

Yes, it was one of those classic moments that when remembered brings laughter with it. Just to be known. What a feeling!

Yes, we all want to "look good" to others. Not proper use of the English language by any means, but you get the idea. But whether we want to admit it or not, we try to put on the best possible front as we want to make a good impression.

I am sure you have asked someone out of politeness how they are doing, and you get an earful of what they are doing, how capable they are, and where they plan on going. Now, I have been guilty of this as much as anybody. My girls told me one time after I had exchanged pleasantries with someone that I shared TMI. "What?" I asked. "TMI, Mother. Too Much Information." So, now as not to embarrass my lovelies, I try to answer, "I'm just fine. And you?"

and leave it at that. This type of practice really takes some effort on my part.

The Bible strongly advises us on this issue in Isaiah 2:11: "The lofty looks of man shall be humbled, and the haughtiness of men shall be bowed down, and the Lord alone shall be exalted in that day." When I have the tendency to make myself look good, I will remember this verse. The Bible, however, does say that we can let our light shine in Matthew 5:16, but only if it will glorify Him: "Let your light so shine before men, that they may see your good works, and glorify your Father which is in heaven."

Now there is nothing wrong with sharing the happenings in your life with others. I love hearing what other people are doing—perhaps because I am a bit nosy. But if we aren't careful, we can take it too far to the point of exalting us instead of exalting Him, the only King and the Lord of lords. We are nothing, but through God we can be something, as long as we keep Him the center of our lives, the center of our universe. And you know, if we exalt Him, or as the Bible says in, "confess" Him before men, He will confess us in Heaven. If we praise Him here, He will reward us in Heaven. We were made to worship Him, and I don't want to ever forget that.

My nephew Geoff is quite a musician and has a band that honors and worships God. I asked Geoff what the name of the band was and he said, "Oh, we just call it MOD for short."

⚮ Are You a Joy Maker?

"MOD?" I asked in confusion. "What exactly does that mean? Because you have a modern sound?"

"Oh, no," he responded. "It's short for Made of Dirt."

Yes, Geoff, you have the right idea. We are made of dirt. God formed us out of the dirt of the earth and made mud balls out of all of us.

Dad was in the hospital and quite ill. He said that he had a substitute doctor come by his room one afternoon to do his hospital call. The doctor was explaining something to him, and my dad couldn't see because his glasses were on a table behind him. He asked the doctor if he could hand his glasses to him, and the doctor arrogantly told him that was not his job. He told my dad to call a nurse. And I thought doctors were supposed to care for the human race. Perhaps he didn't realize that he was just a mud ball.

I don't want to forget that God formed this mud ball and gave me a reason to live. He knows everything about me, and He knows my name. So I hope that every time I might have a moment of "look who I am" that God will remind me that I'm just a mud ball He formed.

Interlude 18

In a Fog

Why do my children insist on being involved with everything they possibly can? This question crosses my mind quite often, especially when I am chauffeuring Kalee to some event that she just *has* to attend. This is the third time that history has repeated itself as I completed the task of chauffeuring my other two daughters to their necessary events. Thankfully, now they are able to drive themselves.

This specific event that Kalee was to attend occurred at 4:00 in the morning. Can you imagine? Being the all-involved person she is, she serves on the Student Council for her freshman class, and the counselor found it necessary that they arrive at that unbelievable hour to blow up balloons. So, I stumbled out of bed to awaken my dedicated child at 3:00 a.m. Of course, we had to allow time to go by and get her an upgraded coffee drink from the local

∽ Are You a Joy Maker?

Quick Trip so she could survive this arduous requirement.

After retrieving the coffee, we started the journey to the school. All of a sudden we were surrounded by a blanket of fog. We could barely see beyond a few feet of our car. This was not a good thing since we live out in the country with only access to two-way traffic. My only salvation was that most intelligent people were at home asleep, which is where everyone should be. However, driving through the fog was quite frightening. Now, I have driven in fog before, so this was not a new phenomenon. But this fog was thick and unyielding—somewhat like my state of mind on this early, early morning.

Of course, as I often do, I applied a spiritual application to this jaunt. How frightening it would be to be so overwhelmed with burdens and cares of life that we cannot even see which way to take. To be blanketed and surrounded by something so light created an ominous feeling to the atmosphere. Even though we had traveled this road many times before, the fog made it difficult for us to get to our destination. Kalee kept saying, "Mom, I know we are lost. This just does not seem right." I kept assuring her we were on the right road, even though at times I was not certain myself. What a relief it was when the gate entrance to the school suddenly materialized out of the fog!

In a Fog

Fog is simply a cloud bank that settles too close to the earth. Wikipedia instructs us that fog reduces our visibility to about one kilometer, and it is very dense. This handy resource also pointed out that it causes shadows to appear. No wonder I thought it was ominous that early morning.[4]

Life is not always an easy road. We are often surrounded by a thick blanket of fog that may even make us question our own faith on the path we are traversing.

Not being able to see where you are going is no fun. My husband tells of the time when he was a little boy and his school teacher noticed he was squinting. He ended up going to the eye doctor and it was discovered that he definitely needed glasses. He said when he first got his glasses, he was amazed at the difference. He would put them on, focus on some point, and say, "There it is!" and then, "Now it's gone." His eyes were exceedingly poor, and his parents felt so badly that they did not know he could not see well. He said that a whole new world opened up to him. He was amazed at how much he had actually been missing because he could not see. It was like he had been in a fog, surrounded by a blur.

We don't always see life with a clear view. There's a bunch of "stuff" that could cloud our vision and keep us from seeing what God has in store for us. At one General Conference, Joan Ewing did a recitation on "Stuff." For her presentation, she

◌ Are You a Joy Maker?

loaded herself down with chains, various scarves, keys, and all kind of things on her body to the extent that it was difficult to walk. And she spoke about becoming so focused on the "stuff" in our lives that we can't see Jesus the way we should. In this day and time, we need a clear view of Jesus in our sights.

Now, as much as I hate to admit it, I am at the age when I need a *little* assistance with my vision. Perhaps I should go beyond a little assistance. Since I love to read, this is a difficult thing for me. I can't read without at least having some type of glasses perched daintily on my nose. (I have to make it sound as delicate as possible since I feel like glasses make me look older.) If I don't have my handy glasses on, it is a complete blur. All the words look like they are in a fog. I know you are deeply touched by my dilemma. It is important to me to do whatever is necessary so that I can see clearly. Thus, I tolerate the glasses.

We should not let the things of this world cloud our vision. Yes, there will always be foggy days that seem impenetrable. But we must keep believing that the fog will soon lift because eventually it always does. So until the fog does lift, keep faith in your life and find something in the denseness to be joyful about. I mean, just think how easy it is to get lost in it, away from all hustle and bustle of the world. I thought that morning when we first walked out to the car how peaceful and tranquil the fog felt. It smelled so refreshing, and I felt a keen sense of well

In a Fog

being. That is, until I started driving it. But I just switched on those old headlights, found out I could see better with them on dim, squinted my beady little eyes, and pressed forward.

The fog remained intact all the way back to the house. But then just as I arrived home, the sun's rays began breaking through the dense fog, and I watched fascinated as the fog rolled away to reveal a beautiful, clear sky. Ah! It was wonderful.

We may encounter a lot of fog in our lives as we press toward the mark. And at times, it seems like we may feel like we are even lost. But just remember, God is even in the fog. He will always be with us. And if we stay steady, He will make the fog lift again. A beautiful sun will come breaking through so that we can see clearly His glory and power: "For now we see through a glass, darkly; but then face to face: now I know in part; but then shall I know even as also I am known" (I Corinthians 13:11-13).

The real voyage of discovery consists not in seeing new landscapes but in having new eyes.
—Marcel Proust

Never fear shadows. They simply mean there's a light shining somewhere nearby.
—Ruth E. Renkel

---

[4] Wikipedia.org/wiki/fog

༄ Are You a Joy Maker?

Courtney with precious Wesley Williams

The girls with friends Felizia Medina and Sharon Martinez

Interlude 19

Shut My Mouth

My family and I were living in St. Louis while my husband served as the Director of Promotions for the Youth Division of the United Pentecostal Church International. Following one Sunday morning church service, several of us were congregated in the foyer visiting. Suddenly, Courtney, our middle daughter, came running up to me and in a loud voice declared loudly, "Mommy, Kara just said the 's' word." A surprised silence reigned at her comment. Aware of what everyone was thinking, I quickly announced, "Oh, our 's' word is 'shut up.'" Laughter followed my rather abrupt explanation. Kids can sometimes share way too much information.

I remember hearing my folks talk about an incident that happened when our good friends, the John Kershaws, pastored in Lubbock, Texas. One Sunday morning, the teacher was taking prayer requests in

☙ Are You a Joy Maker?

the Sunday school class. One little bus-route girl raised her hand and said, "Pray for Daddy 'cause he drinks beer." Susan Kershaw, feeling left out because she never seemed to have a prayer request, raised her hand and said, "Pray for my Daddy. He drinks beer, too." Of course, the teacher realized that she was just trying to fit in and quickly assured the class that the pastor certainly did not drink beer.

How often have we wished we could shut our kids' mouths from sharing some tidbit or other about our lives? They tend to speak evangelistically because they so want to out-do someone's story, even if it means telling a "whopper." I have not only wished my kids would shut their mouths, but I can think of several times I would like to take back some unwise words I may have spoken, wishing I would have just kept my mouth shut.

There is a passage in the Bible that tells us to shut our mouth. Well, maybe it's not said in exactly that manner, but it comes as close as it possibly can. It states, "Even a fool, when he holdeth his peace, is counted wise: [and] he that shutteth his lips [is esteemed] a man of understanding" (Proverbs 17:28). It is so difficult to keep silent when unfair things happen to us, or it is for me anyway. There are probably times the Lord would like to physically shut my mouth like he did Zacharias, the priest. The story that is told in the first chapter of Luke is a favorite of mine. Zacharias and Elisabeth were unable to have children although they had longed for a child. In verse 6, it says, "And they were both righteous before God, walking in all the commandments and ordinances of the Lord blameless" (Luke 1:6). How I would like for someone to write such words about me, but I can tell you now, that will never happen. Since these two righteous people had honored God for so long, He granted their hearts' desire. Gabriel the angel visited Zacharias when he was fulfilling the duties of his priesthood and told him of the coming child. Now, I cannot blame Zacharias, but the Scripture tells us he doubted the prophecy and asked for a sign. I would have doubted the prophecy as well, I am sure. However, since he did doubt, Luke 1:20 says that he was not able to speak until such time as the prophecy came about.

Talk about a trial! It would definitely have been a trial for me to not be able to talk. That would be a very harsh punishment indeed. I am like the little boy after church one Sunday morning who suddenly announced to his mother, "Mom, I've decided I'm going to be a minister when I grow up."

"That's okay with us," the mother said, thinking her son had some spiritual insight. "But what made you decide to be a minister?"

"Well," the boy replied, "I'll have to go to church on Sunday anyway, and I figure it will be more fun to stand up and talk than to sit still and listen."

✎ Are You a Joy Maker?

I wonder how often the Lord would like to take away our speech capabilities. It would especially be a good thing if when someone uses His name in an inappropriate manner that our Lord could just— *kapow*—make them dumb. I think anyone who uses His name in vain is dumb anyway, but the Bible was referring to the fact that Zacharias would not be able to speak.

I hope that the Lord doesn't cringe too much at my words. I hope He doesn't wish he could shut my mouth. However, I'm certain there are many occasions He would like to shut me up. I should well memorize the verse found in Job 6:24 that says, "Teach me, and I will hold my tongue: and cause me to understand wherein I have erred." I want to try my best, with God's help, to speak appropriately and in a good manner.

The Bible gives so much instruction about the tongue and using it wisely, rather than spewing forth anger and discord. Proverbs 15:1 says "A soft answer turneth away wrath, but grievous words stir up anger."

The tongue seems to be the hardest member of the body to tame.

The story of Baalam the prophet fascinates me. This prophet was told by God not to prophesy against the Israelites, but because the princes of Moab offered him numerous gifts and treasure, he decided to go against God's instruction. On the way to prophesy, an angel stood blocking his way. Balaam never saw him, and even whipped the donkey several times trying to get him to move ahead. Then suddenly, the donkey spoke to the cantankerous prophet and saved him from the wrath of God. I hope the Lord doesn't have to use an animal to speak to me. And if He did decide to speak through Sugar, my little black and white dog, I think I would listen the first time, instead of continuing in my wrong ways.

God did tame our tongue when He gave us the precious gift of the Holy Ghost. I want to become more observant and careful about the words I say and the way I speak so that I will please Him. I want to be like Proverbs 31:26: "She openeth her mouth with wisdom; and in her tongue is the law of kindness."

I would much rather that I had kindness in my tongue than for Him to want to shut my mouth because I won't be quiet. Each day I want to make certain that kind words are a part of my vocabulary, instead of making certain I say my piece. I pray the Lord will help me control my tongue, for it would certainly not be a good thing if He shuts my mouth. It would be more than I could bear. I want my mouth to sing His praises and my tongue to speak of His greatness.

◯ Are You a Joy Maker?

"Let the words of my mouth and the meditation of my heart be acceptable in thy sight, O LORD, my strength and my redeemer" (Psalm 19:14).

"A word fitly spoken is like apples of gold in pictures of silver" (Proverbs 25:11).

The family together for a Kodak moment

How ironic that the chattiest women in the world are pictured following this interlude—the daughters and I enjoying General Conference 2009

Interlude 20

Oh, Happy Day!

I drove into our driveway and opened the garage, thankful to at last be at home. I stepped to the back of the vehicle to open the hatch so that I could unload the groceries I had just bought. Intent upon my task at hand, I failed to hear the approach of footsteps.

"Hey, there," said a little girl's voice. I turned to see two of our cute little neighborhood girls.

'Hi, girls!" I said. "How are you today?"

"We're fine," they both chorused in unison.

"Good," I answered. "So what are you two up to today?"

The older one answered, "Do you have two dollars?"

"Oh, hon," I responded. "I don't usually carry cash. I just use my debit card."

A look of confusion crossed her pert little features. She answered, "I said two *daughters*, you know, like your girls."

"Oh, I'm sorry, sweetheart. I thought you said *dollars*." I said. "I have three daughters, in fact. One of my daughters is married."

A grin appeared, "Oh yeah! Does she still live in your house?"

"No, she lives in Memphis now," I answered.

Then she continued, "Could we come in and say 'Hi' to your two daughters that live here then?"

Again, I answered, "I'm sorry, sweetheart. They aren't here. One is at a school play practice and the other is out of town." Disappointment appeared on both their faces. "But you know, you can come back some other time and then come in and say 'hello' to them."

The grins reappeared, "Okay," they said in unison, once again happy. The two little cherubs think my girls are fascinating. They sometimes sit in the yard just so they can catch a glimpse of them as they leave or arrive, dreaming of the day when they can be grown up and do fun stuff, too. I remember well doing the same thing with our neighbor, Phyllis Christian (ironic that our neighbors had the name of *Christian*). My sister and I used to watch her and dream of the day when we would have boyfriends and get to go out all dressed up. That seemed to be the epitome of life. We longed for that happy day.

I continued to carry the groceries in and noticed that the little girls had not left our yard yet. They were whispering together and giggling. Then here they came skipping back up the drive.

Oh, Happy Day!

"Happy Earth Day!" the oldest girl said.
"Happy *what* day?" I asked.
"Happy *Earth* Day!" she said again.

The other little girl spoke up, "You know, we're supposed to celebrate the Earth."

Smiling, I answered, "Oh, I see. Thank you very much." Since I would not consider myself an "earth-type" person, or an environmentalist, I was not overly impressed with this information.

Then the smallest girl whispered quite loudly to the other girl, "I think that Earth Day was the day before yesterday."

The oldest girl answered back, "It doesn't matter. We can still celebrate!"

I continued smiling as I entered the house and bid the two small ones good-bye. What precious gifts children are! I was a bit out of sorts from daily tasking and was only intent on getting everything done so I could relax for a few moments. And in the midst of trying to do just that, I failed to celebrate the day as I should. This April day was indeed one to be celebrated. The weather was lovely, the temperature was just right at 73 degrees, no wind or rain apparent, and the sun shone brightly. And I had failed to give God the proper thanks for this beautiful day. Whether Earth Day or not, it was still a day to celebrate. It was a happy day.

Just like the two little lovelies who dropped by to say hello, we should learn to celebrate each day God has given us. And if there is no reason to celebrate, we should celebrate anyway. We should celebrate the salvation God so willingly gave us. More than anything, I believe He wants us to serve Him with joy and gladness. He wants us to come before His presence with singing. He wants us to be happy and He wants us to have a happy day.

Having a happy day may not always be easy. Paul is a good example of knowing how to handle the adversity of a day. He was brought before King Agrippa by Festus. He was imprisoned and questioned over and over for his beliefs. One verse that caught my attention was Acts 26:2. King Agrippa had just asked Paul to speak for himself, and his first statement was, "I think myself happy, King Agrippa, because I shall answer for myself this day before thee touching all the things whereof I am accused of the Jews."

Now if I was in prison being brought before a ruler or judge for questioning, I don't think I would "think myself happy." Perhaps Paul was having trouble being positive as well and found it necessary to "think himself happy." There are going to be times in your life when happiness is not at all evident. However, we should perhaps follow Paul's example and "think ourselves happy." During a bad day, we should look for the good and count our blessings, even if it means naming them one by one.

Oh, Happy Day!

My husband mentions often his wonderful father and how he was always the encourager. One of his favorite statements to his three rowdy boys when they expressed their boredom was "Make yourself happy." In other words, only you can control whether you are happy or not. I have seen so many base their happiness on material things. They cannot be happy unless they have the latest gadget or the finest car or lots of money.

I saw a cute poem that was entitled "Where Would You Be?" and it went like this:

> Where Would You Be . . .
> If you have all the money your heart desires?
> If you had the most fabulous home in the perfect neighborhood?
> If you had no worries?
> If you came home and the finest gourmet meal is waiting you?
> If your bathwater had been run?
> If you had the perfect kids?
> If your spouse was awaiting you with open arms?
> So where would you be . . .
> Most likely in the WRONG HOUSE!

We cannot buy happiness. We have to "think ourselves happy." The Bible gives us further instruction on happiness in Philippians 4:11 (also authored by the apostle Paul): "Not that I speak in respect of

◯ Are You a Joy Maker?

want: for I have learned, in whatsoever state I am, therewith to be content." I have come to this startling and profound conclusion. (I'm certain no one else has ever thought of this before.) Even though we may not have anything specific to celebrate, just like my two little neighbors, we need to celebrate anyway. We need to "think ourselves happy," and we need to "learn to be content." Happiness doesn't always just happen. We sometimes have to make it happen. And we have to "learn" to be happy. Until we learn to be happy, we won't be happy.

Happiness comes from the Lord who made heaven and earth. One of my favorite old spirituals is entitled "Oh, Happy Day."[5]

Oh, happy day, (repeat)
Oh, happy day, (repeat)
When Jesus washed, (repeat)
When Jesus washed, (repeat)
He washed my sins away.
Oh, happy day, (repeat)
It was a happy day.

Chorus: He taught me how to watch,
watch and pray
And live rejoicing every day, every day.

So, if you are having difficulty finding happiness today, I have made the words very accessible for you. Just break forth into this song, and it should

Oh, Happy Day!

not take very long before you are actually bounding around the room with happiness.

Often when we speak with someone, we will end the conversation with "Have a good day." I think I am going to change my quip to "Have a happy day."

We either make ourselves happy or miserable. The amount of work is the same.
—Carlos Castaneda

---

[5] Public Domain

Are You a Joy Maker?

Banqueting with friends, the David Bernards, the Robert Stroups, the C. Pat Williams, and the Mark Jordans

Another banquet with my dearest husband, Mark

Interlude 21

I Want My Joy Back

As I came up the stairs, I passed the bedroom of my oldest daughter and heard some rather upbeat music reverberating through what seemed to be the entire upstairs. I stopped for a minute and heard the words pounding through the door: "I Want It All Back," written by Tye Tribett. I peered in and watched two of my daughters practicing a sign language drama for one of our Sunday services. They were really involved with the song, so they were unaware of my presence. Now to be perfectly honest, it's not a song that I would probably consider as a solo, nor is it the type of song I grew up with. But then I began to listen to the words: "The battle's not mine, the battle is the Lord's; in the name of Jesus, I'm taking it by force—I want it all back."

Yes, the song definitely will put some "umph" in you. When I think of how diligently the devil works to discourage, to dissuade, to frustrate us, it does tend to make me mad. I think this is perhaps where the Scripture comes in "Be ye angry, and sin not" (Ephesians 4:26). We do have permission to get mad at the devil.

Several years ago while visiting in Austin, Texas, I had to go through an unscheduled brain surgery. Christian Life Church, pastored by Rex Johnson, went out of their way to assist us during this traumatic time, and we made many new friends. One such family that went out of their way for us was Ron and Margo Ferguson. This wonderful couple had a son named Brandon who was the epitome of kindness and integrity. I can still remember the first time I met Brandon. His big smile immediately drew me to this young man. He was the life of the party. The young people looked to him for setting up the place to go eat following service and usually called him to see what was going on with the rest of the youth group. He was friendly with everyone, even the elder members of the church.

Brandon lived in a neighborhood close to my parents and took it upon himself to mow their lawn. He adopted my folks as his grandparents and asked my dad to show him how to tie his tie the way Dad did. He dropped by to check on them, often just at breakfast time so he could have some of Mom's sausage and eggs. This vibrant young man was a joy to be around.

I Want My Joy Back ⁓

On Valentines's Day, Brandon suffered a severe headache, nearly becoming unconscious. He continued to have such spells, and the doctors decided to do further testing. It was discovered that Brandon had a fast-growing malignant brain tumor. A surgery was immediately scheduled and the doctors came with the dire news that they removed the tumor, but with the type of cancer it was, it would most likely grow back very quickly. For approximately three years, Brandon fought with a valiant effort to defeat this disease. For three years, he would try to return to a normal life of college and just being a normal young man. During some of his sickest times, he was not allowed to drive to college, so his dad would take him because he was determined to continue his degree. Between the various surgeries and sicknesses, he would strive to continue. Still, he exuded joy. He was so excited when he completed his college and was hired as a kindergarten teacher at an elementary school.

While I was visiting my family in Austin, Brandon had again found out that the tumor had grown back, and he was suffering so much pain. He was scheduled to be the best man in his friend Brad Wilkinson's wedding. Since he was having difficulty standing, they sat a bar stool on the platform by where Brandon would be standing so he could sit down if he needed. On Saturday following the wedding, they called a special prayer meeting at

༄ Are You a Joy Maker?

Brandon's house because he was so sick. We gathered there and prayed for some time, and then several in the room shared stories to try to encourage Brandon. Finally, one lady said that we needed to pray for specifics and asked Brandon what one thing he really wanted us to pray for specifically. Without hardly any hesitation, he answered, "I want everyone to pray that I will get my joy back."

I was amazed. With all the pain Brandon was suffering, he didn't ask for relief from that or healing for his body. He wanted us to pray that he would get his joy back. Feeling joy was so important to him. More than ever, I was so impressed with this young man and his attitude.

Much to the sadness of so many, Brandon went to be with the Lord a few weeks later on November 21, 2006, at the age of twenty-five. Of course, I along with so many questioned why such an outstanding young man of high character was taken from this life. It seemed so unfair. The grief of his parents, his church family, his friends, and his kindergarten class seemed unbearable. While praying one night for the family, I asked the Lord to help us all be able to understand why he had to leave us. He was so selfless and all he had asked for was that he would get his joy back. In a slow, peaceful way, it came to me that Brandon had indeed regained his joy. I can imagine that when he walked through those pearly gates, our heavenly Father welcomed him with a big bear hug and said, "Welcome to the Joy that lasts forever!" Brandon, you did indeed "get your joy back."

Brandon's Song
by Larry Wilson

I'll remember the look, his grin from ear to ear,
And the way, that he could make you smile,
A heart of gold, so soft and dear,
He was a man that was so strong,
He was a boy that had no fear
No need to say goodbye or ask the question why,
He said it's all become so clear

Don't cry for me, I've been set free,
I'm at the Father's side
No more battles, with this flesh and blood,
This is the reason that Jesus died.
Now in His arms I lay, so safe and sound,
You should hear the angels sing,
Yes, I'll be right here, waiting Mom and Dad,
Me and the Mighty King

Don't consider me gone,
I'm in a better place, if you could see just what I see,
If you could hear the voices of the angels sing,
Then you would wish that you were me,

◯ Are You a Joy Maker?

The streets of gold I walk as I hold His hand,
As He leads me to my home
No more tears I shed, I'm alive not dead,
I'm with Jesus forevermore.

*Joy maker friends—
Brandon Ferguson with my
dad, Jim Bob Smart*

The greatest use of life is to spend it for something that will outlast it.
—William James

Interlude 22

What's Your Story?

We all like to hear a good story. And when sitting in a crowd of friends, the stories can definitely fly around. I count it such an enjoyable endeavor to just swap stories.

My husband is quite a storyteller. He can keep our girls entertained for a long time telling stories of his childhood, church stories, and even better, Bible school stories. And he remembers the stories that his dad told him as a boy of the wild west adventures of his Great, Great, Great Uncle George Mead, who was a horse thief. Old Uncle George even rode one time with Jesse James. Isn't that a proud family heritage? Although that is not something we should be proud of, it is still something of significance since Jesse was quite a famous outlaw. And to think that one of our family members actually met him one time, well, that makes quite a story!

◌ Are You a Joy Maker?

My husband also tells of the time his Uncle George sought shelter in an old, rundown barn during a massive rainstorm. When he entered the premises, he sensed he was not alone. "Howdy," he ventured to the presence. "Howdy," a gravelly voice responded. It was so dark and the storm was so dense, Uncle George said you couldn't see your hand in front of your face. They didn't have anything to start a fire, so it was pitch black. As he settled in for the night and laid his head down on his saddle, he sensed his unknown companion staring at him. He raised up and heard the guy lay back down. All was quiet for a moment and then old Uncle George came awake again, sensing once again he was being watched. Grabbing his gun and raising up slowly, he pointed it in the stranger's direction and stated emphatically, "If you keep doing that, I will leave you here." The threatening voice of our old Uncle George, at least we like to think so, subdued any further actions of the stranger in the night.

Yes, it makes quite an exciting story. And everyone likes exciting stories. And everyone wants their story to be just a bit better than someone else's.

My sister, Vicki, enjoys the opportunity of working with Down syndrome children. While growing up in west Texas, she made friends with a Down syndrome girl named Bobbie. Bobbie was full of life and brought much joy to everyone around her. At our youth camps, she would always find Vicki and follow her around. Bobbie idolized Vicki and made every effort possible to hang out with her and her friends. Vicki visited some friends in Odessa, Texas, one weekend at the church Bobbie attended. The people of the church went out of their way to let Bobbie know they loved and cared about her. During one particular service, the pastor was focusing on the importance of winning people to the Lord, and several had shared their stories. He asked if anyone else had something they would like to share with the congregation. Before Bobbie's mother could stop her, she jumped to her feet and said, "Brother Smelser, I witnessed to thousands and thousands of souls this week." Then she paused, looked around, and realizing that she should not lie, covered her mouth with her chubby little hand, and said, "That's not right!" Little Bobbie just wanted a story of her own and wanted it to be better than everyone else's story.

We are all guilty of wanting a better story. Confession time: I know that sometimes when in a group of storytellers, I will often lose my focus on their stories while thinking of something I could share. It seems we all have something we want to say, or at least I do.

A few years back I took a trip to Austin to see my parents and sister. Since I am not the best flier, I will talk to people, trying to ease my nervousness. I know some people probably think I am a "Chatty Kathy", or rather a "Chatty Karla," but it does help me to remain calm. My husband and the girls say that is just an excuse to find some reason to talk. In this particular incident, I had settled snugly in my seat with the seatbelt all fastened, ready to begin my journey of soaring into the sky. I watched as a tall, dark-haired man placed his bags underneath the seat and sat down. His hair was long, and he was dressed in easy, casual clothing. Of course, I spoke first, which comes as no surprise, I'm sure.

He pulled out the latest innovative cell phone. I glanced at it and made the most profound statement, "That's a nice cell phone."

He glanced at me and agreed, "Yes, I just purchased it, and it is rather nice."

I then added, "Well, I don't know much about the intricate cell phones. I just mainly know how to answer and text."

Then since I seemed interested, he began to show me the various things the phone would do. Although I didn't understand everything he related, I acted as if I thought it was the most awesome mechanism I had ever seen. And, my interest spurred the man on to talk.

We discussed several things, and then I asked, "So what kind of work do you do?"

He then proceeded to tell me that he was an electrical engineer and worked for a company that developed gadgets for the Defense Department. Well, the story he related was intriguing! He talked about a certain gadget he helped developed that was shaped like a disk that soldiers could throw into a building before entering themselves. This impressive mechanism would pinpoint the location of enemy soldiers by throwing off some kind of red beam in their direction. It sounded phenomenal! He shared several other fascinating things, and I was so impressed! Of course, I cannot remember all the details he shared, but it was quite remarkable to talk to the man. Then he looked at me and said, "So what do you do?"

Okay, now. Here I've been listening to this brilliant man for some time, and I certainly did not want to appear inept or unintelligent. So how do I answer? "I'm a minister's wife." Or "I am mainly a homemaker and do a little writing on the side." Such a dilemma I found myself in. Then I had an epiphany!

"Oh," I answered nonchalantly, "I'm an author." How rewarding it was to see the interest that flooded his countenance! Now let me insert something here. I had just had my first book approved for publication. Nothing had been published yet at that time, but I wasn't lying. I was an author! And what would you have done? I mean I couldn't say, "Oh, I'm a mom," or, "I work part-time as a secretary." That wouldn't have been impressive at all. I wanted my story to at least be somewhat intriguing since he seemed to have more intelligence in one little finger

◯ Are You a Joy Maker?

than I had in my whole brain. I wanted my story to at least be a good one.

So everyone has a story. Some have great stories and some have mediocre stories. Some have not so good stories. Some have suffered untold hardships in their lives, while others seem to have an easier road to travel. However, no one is immune from the struggles life hands us.

I often look at people and think, "They are so fortunate. It seems like everything goes their way." But appearances can be deceiving. While at an Arkansas ladies conference, I had the opportunity to hear Janice Sjostrand. And she always has quite a story to tell. She talked about her chance to sing at the inauguration of President Clinton some years back. I recalled watching the DVD and hearing her sing "We Are Standing on Holy Ground" with such vibrancy and feeling. And I remember thinking, "Wow, she has it made! Singing at an inauguration with millions watching—what an accomplishment! A once-in-a-lifetime opportunity. She is so lucky."

However, the day she sang at that inauguration was quite the opposite for her. She told of how her young daughter became deathly ill and they could not figure out what was wrong with her. The president's physician was called in and suggested she be taken to the hospital. No one seemed to have a diagnosis for the child. They were not even certain she would be all right. So while Sister Sjostrand was singing that day, her little girl lay in the hospital with an uncertain future. It was not at all as it appeared to be. Thankfully, her daughter came through and just recently was given the good news that her disease was in remission. That's Janice Sjostrand's story.

The greatest story ever told is one of the greatest lives ever lived. Jesus came, clothed in the form of a babe, grew up in a non-descript town in a poor carpenter's shop, spent three years ministering and performing unbelievable miracles, became what we would consider "known" for just a short period of time, and then was arrested for no apparent reason at all. He was beaten, ridiculed, spat upon, and brought before Pilate who released a murderer instead of Him. He was executed in the worst possible way, and all seemed lost when He died.

But that is not the end of His story. In three days, He arose from the grave, victorious over death. There is a poem that says: "All the armies that have ever marched, all the navies that have ever sailed, all the rulers that ever reigned on this earth, have not affected the lives of men on earth like this one solitary life." His story was a miracle!

So the story of your life may not be a fairy tale. Your handsome prince or princess may have turned out just the opposite. Your status may not be one of wealth and success. But God's knows your story, and He cares deeply what happens to your story. Whatever may have happened thus far in your story, the

◯ Are You a Joy Maker?

most important part is that you can determine the ending. If you serve God with all your mind and soul, there will be a happy ending for you, better than any fairy tale you have ever heard. That makes your story a great one! So, live your story with hope! Live your story with peace! And most of all, live your story with joy!

Tell me the story of Jesus,
Write on my heart every word,
Tell me the story most precious,
Sweetest that ever was heard.

—Fanny Crosby

Janice Sjostrand and I
arriving at
a ladies conference
dressed in the same attire
and still laughing